C000258129

More Tales

from a

Cornish Lugger

Paul Greenwood

30127 07602575 3

© Paul Greenwood 2011

All rights reserved. No part of this publication may be reproduced or transmitted in any form or by any means, electronic or mechanical, including photocopying, recording, or any information storage or retrieval system, without prior permission in writing from the publisher. The right of Paul Greenwood to be identified as the author of this work has been asserted by him in accordance with the Copyright, Designs and Patents Act 1988.

British Library Cataloguing in Publication Data.
A catalogue record for this book is available from the British Library.

ISBN 978-0955954191

Published by
Polperro Heritage Press,
Clifton-upon-Teme, Worcestershire WR6 6EN UK
www.polperropress.co.uk

Cover design
Simon Hammond

Printed by
Orphans Press, Leominster
HR6 0LD UK

Suffolk County Council	
30127 07602575 3	
Askews & Holts	May-2011
639.2092	£7.95

Contents

By the same author

ONCE ABOARD A CORNISH LUGGER

I dedicate this book to those who never returned

What cost to us, the fishermen,
The toilers of the sea,
To dare old Mother Nature
And bring home fish to thee.

"The price of fish,"
"The cost of fish,"
A housewife to me discerned...

Well, weigh your cost with the children
Whose fathers never returned.

[Mark Curtis, Newlyn skipper]

Introduction

Cornwall, a county officially classed as the poorest in England, especially in the winter time, with high unemployment and a very low average wage, generally makes for pretty grim reading. For years now the place has been marketed as a sort of Disneyesque theme park, a land of myth and legend, of smugglers and pirates, mining and fishing, most of it now safely locked into the past.

The industries that once earned so many people in this county a living have slipped, or are slipping away. The mines, unable to compete with foreign competition but still rich in tin, copper, lead and silver now lie silent and overgrown, and the men who once worked them relocated to hard rock mines all over the globe. While today, farmers take part time jobs to keep the wolf from the door and many have converted their barns into holiday accommodation.

Global competition has led to massive job cuts in the once mighty china clay industry, while European government policy ensures that the fishing fleet continues to shrink. All but a handful of the boatyards have closed down, their now oh so desirable waterside locations cleared to make way for luxury flats that will overlook yet another marina; their skilled workforce scattered to make a living elsewhere as car park attendants or building site chippies. The only traditional industry still thriving, though I doubt the Cornish play much of a part in it nowadays, is smuggling: cheap booze and tobacco is not hard to come by, while in the quiet coves and bays, cargoes of illegal drugs must be coming ashore by the ton.

It would seem that just to survive in their own county, many Cornish people have few options but to attend to the tourists and be thankful for their little low paid seasonal jobs. Meanwhile every quaint cottage becomes a holiday home, snapped up at prices that no local could possibly afford. Many villages now have no communities other than a transient population of Home Counties 4+ 4 drivers, plump and pink and resplendent in their smart seaside casuals.

And if funding can be secured, once the last of the smelly fishing boats have gone, many harbours have plans for marinas, complete with posh restaurants and art galleries.

Cornwall always was the poor relation of England, but what little it did have was at least real. Today it is still the poor relative but now, with the way industry is evaporating, the county will soon be trying to earn a living with little more to purvey than myths and legends and the beauty of its scenery. This seems to be the fate of Cornwall, and maybe we should be thankful that at least the place has the tourism when all else is failing. And if, by chance, a wealthy entrepreneur was to appear on the scene with a master plan that would create 3,000 jobs on the south Cornish coast throughout the winter months; one that didn't involve millions of pounds of funding, retraining, or despoiling the entire area, then that man would be hailed as a genius, a hero. But in the late 1960s and early 1970s, that's exactly what did happen, though without the aid of a wealthy businessman or massive grants, and in wintertime, created and run entirely on private enterprise. It was the great Cornish mackerel fishery. From a very doubtful beginning it grew and flourished beyond all expectations, and then it was allowed to fade away. I witnessed at first hand its inception and its demise, and it makes me feel at best, sad; at worst very angry at what was allowed to happen. We who were in that industry had it swept from under our feet, and we stood by helpless and unhelped as our hard-won enterprise was left to die.

I wrote my first book, *Once Aboard A Cornish Lugger*, to record the way of life in the last years that those pilchard fishing boats were operating. But after 45 years working out of the port of Looe as a fisherman, boatman and charter skipper, I now look back and realise that so much else has changed in that time, perhaps I should try and tell that story as well. Because the way of life as I knew it has gone and will never return. In the winter time we went commercial fishing, and there was usually plenty of fish to catch and the freedom to do so. Come the spring time, we painted up our sea-worn wooden boats to take the summer visitors out on pleasure trips. The seasons came and went, and I believe we thought that it would go on forever.

1

Mackerel & Pilchards

On a winter's afternoon early in 1966 the Looe lugger *Iris* entered port from an exploratory day's fishing with about a hundred stone of prime mackerel on her deck. Big beautiful fish like miniature tuna, and on Plymouth fish market the next morning they made the excellent price of £1 per stone. For the five crew members this meant the best part of a week's wage had been put together in one go, a very good day's work indeed. I remember this incident well because I was one of the crew and, like all the other drifter liners, we had been scratching about trying to earn a living with the nets and lines, and believe you me in the winter time it was usually an awful lot of har labour for a very meagre reward.

There was rarely a profit to be made, it was purely an exercise to try and keep the wolf from the door, and he was clawing at the paintwork for most of the time. But a chance remark had given our skipper the idea that there might be a few mackerel about off Plymouth Sound. Why, we had no idea. They had never been there before, but as there was nothing to lose, a hand line consisting of 40 fathoms of cod line ending with a dozen feathered hooks and a pound lead was made up for each man, and early one morning we slipped away on the tide to investigate this rumour. A hundred stone of fish at £1 a stone was excellent money, and if we could do something like that three or four days a week, not only would the wolf be kept from the door, you wouldn't be able to catch a glimpse of him with a pair of powerful binoculars. But who knows with fishing, there may not be a fish to be caught on the next trip out.

The weather held fine for the next few days and on each of those days we found the mackerel and landed a catch, the price staying steady at a £1 a stone on Plymouth market. Of course the other skippers had kept a close eye on what the *Iris* was doing, and when our bit of success looked to be more than a one off, the other four drifters in the port got their hand lines made up ready to have a go themselves. So now there were five boats out hunting about: joining the *Iris* were the *Our Boys*, *Our Daddy*, *Guide Me* and the *Endeavour*, each at the end of the day landing good quality fish, and what was more, the buyers continued to pay good money for it. And so we fished on like this until March when the shoals faded away and eventually there was none to be found. But what an unexpected bonus we had earned. For the first time in years the crews on the boats had earned a decent living wage in the winter months. Would the mackerel return again the following year? We sincerely hoped so.

The following March the pilchard shoals returned to the Cornish coast once more. Not, at first, in any huge numbers but enough to make a bait up for the long lines. So once again we were doing 24 to 30 hour trips out deep in the Channel shooting and hauling seven thousand hooks on seven miles of line, to catch ray, conger, ling etc. That was a nasty shock to the system after weeks of tiddling around up and down the shore with a twelve hook hand line.

By the month of May the pilchard shoals became much more prolific; the long lines could now be put ashore and in their place we hauled aboard the full summer fleet of 22 drift nets, being eleven fathoms deep and nearly two miles long. Night after night we shot and hauled them to supply fish to the cannery at Newlyn. It was all done by sheer muscle power. A big catch could mean eight or ten hours work non stop. That was what it took just to get the fleet of nets back aboard the boat, never mind steaming home, boxing up and landing. In the summer season we also took visitors out shark fishing, a daytime job to go with the night time one we already had. The money was good but sometimes you thought you were going to die on your feet from lack of sleep.

And so October came when once again the pilchard shoals thinned away from the coast and the nets were hauled ashore, dried and stowed back up in the net loft for another winter. Of course the big question then was whether the mackerel shoals would be around again or would we have to spend yet another winter working out of Brixham, living aboard the boat while trying to scratch a living with the herring nets and long lines. We hoped for the former for the latter was a rather grim prospect. So before the herring nets were made ready the hand lines were put aboard to give them a try first, and we weren't disappointed. Up off Plymouth Sound, there they were again, lines full of great big fat mackerel, as bold as brass and as lively as dolphins. Another decent winter season looked to be in prospect.

This sort of work was a real novelty to us because, when a good week's wage was made working the nets and long lines, we were utterly shattered from the sheer physical louster involved, working both by night and day. Rest was something that was taken when the weather turned poor or when we were all on the verge of collapse. And yet there we were, working up and down the shore jigging a little hand line around for the day, home to bed every night and money at the end of the week. It was almost too good to be true.

The boats that first went fishing for mackerel were the ageing survivors from the once mighty Cornish drifter fleet. The oldest were motorised vessels from the days of sail such as the *Guide Me* and the *Our Boys*; others like the *Iris*, *Our Daddy* and the *Eileen* had been auxiliaries, built with both motor and sail for the boom times after WW1. These boats were 38 to 45 feet long and fully decked, fine sea-kindly old craft. I say sea-kindly rather than seaworthy because at the time most of these boats were well on towards the end of their working life. They were safe enough because they were well handled by men who knew them, but after years of hard times and frugal maintenance I dread to think what a surveyor might have had to say about some of them.

The other class of boats then on the coast were what was known as quatters, mainly built for the boom in the fishing after WW2. They were 30 to 38 feet in length, with a long foredeck and a full width open-backed wheel house. The working area was a hatch board deck set about waist high down from the rail. They could be fitted out for whatever fishing was good at the time or worked by one man for the pleasure boating in the summertime. Very versatile and economical craft to work, their big disadvantage was that because they were open, every drop of water that came aboard had to be pumped out, by hand of course. And because of the way things were at the time most of these boats were used only in the summer months for pleasure angling; during the winter the skippers got a job ashore, labouring for a builder, painting and decorating or whatever would bring in a week's wage.

But not this winter. Hand lines were made up and boats that hadn't been to sea in the winter time for many years, were out joining in the bonanza. Roles were really being reversed. To make up the crews, painters and decorators, masons, chippies and shipwrights were going to sea for the winter instead of the fishermen coming ashore. The word was out: something new was happening, and coves and quays that had lain dormant for years were coming back to life as shoals of mackerel came in to winter all along the south Cornish coast. Here was a brand new fishery; from catching to marketing there was much to learn and develop, and many new ideas to try out. One of the first things that had to be improved was the hand line itself.

Hauling by hand all day long led to the twine of the back line cutting into your hands, and when shaking the fish off, the hooks nipped into your hands. It was as bad as drift netting, hands raw and sore with pus-swollen fingers. And of course the line itself was difficult to keep running clear, coiled down onto the deck or into a fish box; the wind could and did blow it about, or a fish would land in it, flapping madly, reducing a carefully flaked down line to a birds nest tangle. The leads on the end of the line weren't really heavy enough either and if you jigged the line for just a bit too long the mackerel on the hooks would swim about with it, so when it was lifted aboard instead of a nice string of fish there was something that resembled a big bunch of bananas, the line and hooks all wound up in one tight ball. All this of course had to be cleared before the line could be dropped again. After this had happened to someone three or four times on the run, it would reduce them to a teeth-gnashing fury, ready to bite lumps out of the mast with sheer frustration. A few neatly worded jibes could prove most entertaining.

Various ideas were tried out to improve the working of the lines, but the first real break-through was made by Tommy Paul, a Londoner who along with his merry crew worked an old Thames Bawley out of Looe called the *Onward*. They appeared at sea one Sunday morning with the peddle crank section of a bicycle frame married to a car wheel. Each man had one of these contraptions clamped to the rail of the boat; the line was wrapped around the wheel and when paid out it was retrieved again by turning the peddle. Of course everyone had a damn good snigger at the *Onward*'s crew as they suffered back turns, over ride, and as many tangles as anyone working a hand line.

Tommy and his gang weren't rated very highly as fishermen and this performance only proved what a gang of cowboys they really were. That was until they ironed out the teething problems and started to work two to one against a hand line. Then it was a different story entirely. All of a sudden there was a rush to copy, or improve on Tommy's invention. Many variations were tried out and most of them worked, until by about 1969 the final form of the 'gurdy' came into being. This was a simple device, a wooden wheel made of half jointed 2x2, 18 inches in diameter with deep V's cut into the end of each of the four arms onto which the line could be wound. A central axle bolt held it to an angle iron stanchion that was clamped to the boat's rail. The wheel was turned by a handle mounted on one of the wheel arms and a fairlead guided the line into place. No more wind blowing the line about and no more fish dancing amongst it. The business end of the line went from a dozen feathered hooks on light gut to double that number with coloured plastic lures all mounted on heavy duty nylon, terminating in a three pound lead, and in those days there were mackerel around big enough to actually swallow these leads.

The fish were still hauled aboard and shaken off by hand, and by that I don't mean that we caught hold of the shank of each hook and tiddled at it until the fish fell off. No, an arm span of line was lifted up and brought down with a whop, jerking six or eight fish off at a go. But by now we protected our hands with heavy industrial plastic gloves which didn't stop all injuries but certainty prevented about 90 per cent. Hooks pricking into the hands were still an all day occurrence, but suffering the agony of having to rip a hook out that had gone in past the barb was greatly reduced. And to keep the line flowing free over the boat, lengths of four and six inch plastic drain pipe were split back and sprung onto the rails, while other lengths were hung over the side between rail and waterline. All this ensured that foul ups were kept to a minimum. We now had the right gear for the job, and catch rates shot up from 100 stone a boat to 100 stone plus per man, in many cases very much more than that.

When the big mackerel were shoaling high in the water, a catch of more than 1,000 stone was not unusual for a smart four-handed crew. Often, with the 30 foot open class of boat, the boat of choice for many of the mackerel men, it was not a question of how much you could catch, but how much you dared haul aboard and remain seaworthy in the weather conditions prevailing on the day. I can't recall a mackerel boat ever foundering, but on fine weather days I have seen them loaded to the point where a good steep wash from a passing merchant ship would have given them serious problems. And to avoid being swamped in poor weather when steaming home, boxes of fish would sometimes have to be dumped overboard to lighten her up a bit and enable the boat to lift more readily to the seas.

Given the amount of fish available to be caught and the size of the boats used to catch them, the catching capacity was as good as it could be. Any better and I think a boat or two would have ended up paying a visit to Neptune.

2

Hand-lining

By the early 1970s the Cornish handline mackerel fishery was expanding at a fantastic rate; it was proving to be very lucrative and very easy to get in on. In those days fishermen had the freedom of the seas. You could buy a boat, any boat, register it and the rest was up to you; the rules, regulations and restrictions were very few indeed.

So, wherever boats were for sale, fishermen from Cornwall were snapping them up. Scotland and Brittany were two good sources of second hand craft, while here in Cornwall just about anything that floated was pressed into service: summer pleasure steamers and ferry boats, wartime motor launches, motor yachts and retired lifeboats. As a rule of thumb, the more motley the boat then the more motley were the men that crewed them. Farm workers, dock-yardies, hippies, barmen and waiters from the hotels, everyone was out there having a go. And why not; it was much better than the dole and it cost very little to fit out a boat for the job. As you can imagine, many of these types dropped out as quickly as they dropped in, but others persevered and many of them went on to become good fishermen. We laughed at a lot of these people, but in a fishery boom you can't suddenly find hundreds of skilled fishermen; the extra manpower has to come from somewhere as boat numbers had gone from twenty or so at the start to over four hundred in a very short space of time.

It was not only second hand boats that were in demand. This boom had given the local boat yards full order books because many of the top fishermen invested in powerful new boats. One or two of these new craft were made of fibre glass, but at the time very little was known about that medium so most skippers stayed with wood. Plus, of course, all around the Cornish coast there were still plenty of boatyards building in wood to a very high standard. On bad weather days there were always car loads of fishermen jaunting off to have a look at some one's new boat then under construction.

All these new boats had to be adaptable to work the different seasons. In Looe they were nearly all of the forward wheelhouse hatch board deck design, able to carry a small hydraulic winch for the stop gap trawling season between the end of the mackerel fishing and the start of summer pleasure angling. In other ports they preferred an aft wheelhouse and a laid deck because they went crabbing, netting or long lining in the summer. And these new boats were a very good investment. There were loans and grants available to help defray the cost, and at the time it was reckoned that a new boat could be paid off within three years.

The mackerel boats of the 1970s and the trawlers and netters that were launched in the 1980s were to be the last hurrah for the wooden boat however. Of course the marketing side of things was expanding rapidly to match the landings of this ever increasing fleet, for what had once been a purely local affair had, by the early 1970s, become very big business. In mackerel landing ports such as Newlyn, Falmouth, Mevagissey and Looe, teams of packers stood by each evening ready to box and ice the day's catch before loading up the waiting refrigeration lorries that carried this fresh Cornish produce to the fish markets of all the major cities in the UK as well as to France, Spain, Italy and Greece. When the weather was fine and the fishing heavy, these packing teams would be working right through the night. Many is the time they would still be boxing and icing the previous day's catch when we were going to sea the following morning.

The catch rate for mackerel had increased tenfold, and it was also hard physical work. Depending on where the fish were to be found it could involve some very long hours. But no fisherman worries about a fifteen or eighteen hour working day if there are fish to be caught. You can have a rest when the winter storms roll in and it's double ropes out to hold the boats to the quay.

Compared with fishermen of today we led a life of great freedom. There was no one telling you what you could or could not fish for; the boat that you went to sea in and the engine that powered it was entirely your business. Each skipper worked the different seasons of the year as he saw fit, old men, young men, old boats and new. But they have all gone now, the boats, the men and the seasons that they worked. These were my main working years and I witnessed it all from the decks of the various boats that I worked on, fair weather and foul, good times and bad, shipwreck and tragedy. It's a tale that any fisherman from my era could tell, but I doubt that they will, so I shall try to put the story together as I saw it while working from the port of Looe.

3

'Doodle Bugs'

In 1973 I returned home to Looe after two and a half years away working as bo'sun on the sailing schooner *Malcolm Miller*. It had been a wonderful experience, but it was all sea time and boozing when ashore, which was fun while it lasted but I didn't want to make a career out of it. Returning home, I bought a thirty foot converted ship's lifeboat and with that I worked in the summer months taking visitors on day trips to Fowey and Polperro, combined with inshore angling trips and evening conger fishing. She was a handy little boat for the summer trade, but just wasn't stout enough for winter work out on the mackerel. So, smartly painted up and all in good working order I put her up for sale, and as luck would have it I soon found a buyer.

After life on the schooner, sailing all around Europe, I felt restless back in Looe. By the spring of 1974 I had money in the bank but no boat to earn a living with and was casting about wondering what I was going to do. I was very tempted to go back sailing on the schooners, but thankfully I managed to talk myself out of it. The question of what to do next however was answered by the sad and untimely death of Theo Matthews, one of the local boatmen. Theo and his son Collin each had a fleet of six, of what in Looe were known as 'doodle bugs', 14 foot clinker built boats powered by a small inboard engine, hired out to the summer visitors at an hourly rate on a self drive basis. This form of boating was very popular and a very good earner, so when Theo's widow put his boats up for sale I jumped at the opportunity to buy them. But this was a branch of boating I knew nothing about. At a first glance it looked a very leisurely way to make a living, sitting in a deck chair on the quayside sunning yourself while taking money from people having an hour's spin around the bay or up the river in one of your boats.

But it wasn't quite like that. Fortunately Collin was there to show me the basics of the business, such as how to maintain and keep the little two stroke engines running, how to raft up the boats to get them on and off their moorings, in fact there were a thousand and one things to learn that I had never come across before. And yes, there was good money to be earned with them, but on a busy day you just never stopped running about.

A typical day on the 'doodle bugs' would start at about eight o'clock in the morning when the boats would be rafted up and brought from their mid-river moorings to the quayside steps that you worked from. The first job was to go from boat to boat with an old brass hand pump and pump them all dry. Next they had to be fuelled up and the engines checked over, sumps drained out, spark plugs cleaned etc. Then the bottom boards and fore decks were scrubbed and the seats wiped down, by which time the boats were ready for the day's work. On the quay we had an old van in which we kept petrol cans, engine spares, fishing lines and tools, a sort of ready-made store for all the things needed to keep the boats running. It was also where my grub tin and flask of tea were kept plus a deckchair I had pinched from the beach, so with everything ready to go there was just time for a slurp of tea and a sit down before the rush began.

Over the school summer holidays, the really busy times, each boatman employed a boy to help out. They were paid about £1 a day, and it was a fine job for a lad, out in the sunshine all day playing on boats. My first helper was Richard Newman. He was about ten or eleven years old and a good little worker. But he was the same as all the other lads; if the day was a bit slack they would get bored and then they would all gang up together and get stroppy and very cheeky. The answer to that problem was to await your moment and grab one of them and hurl him overboard. This treatment served to remind them for a while of where they really stood in the pecking order of things and, if it never actually cured them for long, we gained great satisfaction and amusement at the Doppler effect of the howl they uttered as their little bodies carved an arc through the air before hitting the water with a mighty splash.

Around ten o'clock the first holiday makers would start strolling down the quay and the touting would begin: "Boat Sir, self-drive, a lovely day for a trip up the river or out in the bay," was the usual sort of blag. And if all went well young Richard would be rushing down the quay wall ladder to start a boat and bring it in to the steps. I would see the people aboard, give them a few instructions on the engine and how to steer, take the money (then it was £1 a hour) and away they would go. The boats could carry up to six people so it was pretty good value for money.

On a fine sunny summer's morning all the boats could be away one after another and the pattern for the day would be set: a boat would return, Richard would be there to see it in and help the people off as I would be waiting on the quay with another family, money paid and ready to go.

When the tide turned, ebbing away from the quay, the boats would be anchored off in the stream of the river and we would work from the shingle bank getting the people on and off the boats via a couple of wooden boxes to keep their feet dry. And when the tide crept back in again we would work our way back to the steps once more. Around five o'clock trade would almost come to a halt as everyone went home for their tea, and often that was the time to call a halt to the day ourselves. But if the weather looked set fair, it was often worthwhile to stay for the evening trade, working on until dusk descended around half nine or ten o'clock.

It wasn't always plain sailing though. Some days were utter chaos from one end to the other, with boats stuck on the mud up the river, or stranded on rocks out in the bay. There were times when you would be rushing about trying to do so many things at once you would all but disappear up your own backside. But by mid September the holiday season was all but over, the tourists had returned home and the town was quiet once more. Even the hurdy-gurdy man returned to his winter quarters in Penzance. I can't recall his name, but for many years he tramped the length and breadth of the county pushing a two-wheeled cart, the hurdy-gurdy mounted on top and his camping gear slung underneath. He would always spend a day or so in Looe, stopping in likely spots around the town, his giant musical box producing a near forgotten fairground sound, loud and mechanical, playing songs from the Gilbert & Sullivan operettas and the music halls. He cranked the handle, busking for whatever money people threw into his box. He and a gypsy that toured about in a green horse-drawn caravan must have been among the very last of the itinerants.

Then it was time to put our hard-worked and somewhat battered little motor boats back in their shed for the winter months, elsewhere in Looe shops and cafés would be putting up their shutters. Most of the small pleasure boats were craned ashore and sheeted over, while the bigger craft, those from about twenty five feet and upwards would be making ready for the winter mackerel fishery. Most of the men who worked the 'doodle bugs' and small pleasure boats went to sea on the mackerel boats in the wintertime, and there would be many shore workers getting ready to join the boats as crewmen with this profitable, and ever increasing fleet.

4

'Nibblo' & 'Bonzo'

In the winter of 1974 I had shipped on the *Prosperity*, a fine craft that had been built in Scotland some twenty years before and was about forty feet long. She was fully decked and had a cruiser stern, an aft wheelhouse and was powered by a 70 h.p. Gardner engine, owned and skippered by Bonzo Butters. Also sailing with Bonzo was his brother Nibblo who in the summer time was a speedboat driver. Bonzo and Nibblo, whose real names were Lewis and Harold, were both in their middle to late forties and came from an old Looe family, all their forefathers having been fishermen and sailors. In height, neither one of them topped the five feet mark, though by the thickness of a fag paper Nibblo claimed he was the taller of the two. In build they were both pretty stocky, and personality wise, well, lurking beneath a very spiky and defensive exterior they were as good as gold, but fight and argue!! I had never seen the likes of it until I shipped up with them. It was like going to sea with a pair of human Jack Russell terriers.

Summer being over we were now eager to get the *Prosperity* ready for the winter fishery. Off the boat and into the store went the summer paraphernalia: the shark chair, the fishing rods and bench seats followed by the sharpie mizzen and the chemical toilet.

And out from the store we dragged, and then shipped up, the heavy pound boards. These were about a foot deep and were fitted both across the beam of the boat and fore and aft so as to divide the deck up into small areas or pounds, thus preventing the catch from sliding about as the boat rolled and plunged at sea. Next, the gaff mizzen was bent on to its spars. This sail, when hoisted and working in conjunction with the engine, would keep the boat riding comfortably head to wind in even the worst of weather, vital when we were working on deck. Where each crewman worked his line, a ten foot length of plastic drainpipe that had been sawn down its length was sprung into the rail. At sea, a corresponding length was slung over the side on ropes between the rail and waterline to stop the hooks from fouling on the hull when the line were being worked. The gurdies had been wire-brushed and oiled up, all free running and ready for action, while plenty of spare sets of feathers and leads had been stowed in the wheelhouse lockers. Oilskins, aprons and sea boots were hung in the engine room where they would keep warm and dry. Last of all we hauled several stacks of fish boxes down from the fish market and stowed them in the deck pounds. Nibblo shopped for a few stores as Bonzo and I topped up the fuel tanks, and that was it. The good ship *Prosperity* along with her gallant crew stood ready to do battle.

"What time in the morning, Bonz?" asks Nibblo.

"I don't know, what do you reckon?" says his brother.

"Well there's been a few fish out the back of the radar buoy, I suppose we could start there and see what happens," comes the reply.

"Yes, that sounds okay, better make it five o'clock then. That alright with you, Captain?" says Bonzo.

In the three years that I sailed on the *Prosperity* I don't think I was ever called by my name. It was 'Captain' from Bonzo, and 'Ned', a nickname I had had for many years, from Nibblo.

"That will do," I reply.

"Right then, five o'clock it is, and don't be late," says Bonzo.

"Huh, who do you think you're talking to, you look out for your own clock, I'll be there," snaps Nibblo.

"'Ark to that little fucker," says Bonzo, addressing me. "I have seen you late plenty of times Nibblo."

"No you fucking haven't."

"Yes I fucking have."

"Ahh, bollocks to you Bonzo, you can poke the Prosperity up your arse if you are going to carry on like that."

Things are starting to get out of hand so I chime in: "For fuck's sake cut it out you pair, five o'clock will do us, and I'll see you then."

With that the situation is defused. "Okay, Captain, and don't be late" says Bonzo, looking at me sideways with a devilish twinkle in his eye. One thing about working on the *Prosperity* was that whatever we did, or whatever decisions had to be made, there was always a full crew debate on it before a conclusion was drawn.

Come the morning we are all aboard on time, thank God, and along with the rest of the Looe fleet we steer out SSW for a couple of hours to bring us out south of the radar buoy. What this buoy has to do with radar and why it is there no one seems to know. It marks nothing and is in deep water, but it had become a handy reference point.

Bonzo eases the engine down now with one eye on the echo sounder and one ear cocked to the VHF. The hunt was on. The mizzen is hoisted and the gurdies are clamped onto the rail, with leads and feathers bent on ready to go. All we need now is a 'scry', a big mark on the sounder, or a shout on the VHF that someone is into fish, but so far nothing much is happening. There are little bits of marks every now and then on the sounder, but when you give them a try there is nothing worth having, just a few small and medium mackerel and not many of them.

"Fucking good start to the season," says Bonzo.

"Don't you worry," says Nibblo. "We shall have them in a minute, I can feel it in my water."

"Well, all I hope is that your water can do better than this echo sounder," Bonzo replies. "Anyway, let's have another cup of tea."

"Another cup of tea! I've made three on the way out already. Any more and you'll piss yourself," comes the retort.

"Nibblo, if I want a cup of tea I'll have one."

"Well, you had better go down forward and make the bastard thing yourself. What do you think I am aboard of this boat, your servant?"

"Servant? You little twat, you aren't smart enough for that."

Oh look out, I think to myself, here they go again.

"Right, I am going down to put the kettle on," I shout. "You don't want a cup then, Nibblo?"

"Of course I do, Ned, I just wasn't going to be seen running around after that short-arsed little fucker in the wheelhouse there."

But arguing about it was as near as we got to that brew of tea, for as we spoke the prop was suddenly thrashing astern and Bonzo was winding up the throttle to bring the boat to halt, shouting "Down lines, a big mark here on the meter."

Nibblo and I paid our hooks over the side and let the lead carry them down into the depths, the arms of our gurdies rotating around like miniature windmills.

"Look out boys, here they are, this feels like the right stuff," shouts Nibblo as both our lines hit into the fish that were shoaling ten fathoms or so beneath our keel. A quick jig on the line to make sure it was full, and the upward wind begins. Twenty-five large and lively mackerel, weighing about two pounds each or more can put up quite a fight especially if they happen to try and dive together, but come up they must, and we were soon lifting strings of these beautiful fish aboard.

An arm span of fish is lifted chest high then brought down with a 'whap' and the catch flies off, blood and slime splattering everywhere, while the tails of gasping fish rap out a tattoo on the deck. Three goes like that and the line is clear, released, and the lead takes it down for more. With a kick ahead now and then on the engine, the old boat rides comfortably on her mizzen, head up to the light westerly breeze. What a start to the season. This is excellent fishing, and to make the best of it the three of us toil away as if being urged on by the Devil himself. The chatter on the VHF has at last ceased, and scattered all around us, boats from Looe, Polperro and Mevagissey are also hauling aboard string after string of big glittering mackerel.

When the fishing was like that, time had no meaning. You stop briefly to clear a tangle in the line, or to pull a fouled hook out of your glove or oilskin and then on you go. It is not until the mackerel are lying on the deck so thick that you are no longer able to shuffle up and down the few feet of deck needed to work the line that a brief halt has to be called. This might be the time for the man nearest the cabin hatch to slip down and put the kettle on, while the fish are hosed down and scooped into boxes or pounds to clear the working area. If a line needs changing or several hooks and lures are missing, now is the time to cut it off and bend on a new set. A quick sandwich and a mug of tea and on we go again, total stop time fifteen minutes, maybe less. That is a luxury. On some boats they only stop to scoop the fish. All afternoon we haul aboard line after line of jumbo mackerel. The boxes are stacked up brim full, and the deck pounds are topped off level with the rail, our backs are aching, our hands are sore and everything not covered in mackerel is cascading with a thick layer of bloody slime and scales including our oilskins and faces.

There is one minor diversion during the afternoon when Nibblo suddenly shouts out: "I've got the bastard, look out here he goes." He has caught a shark and his line was now paying out at a terrific rate.

I have seen plenty of sharks played on a gurdy, but I have never ever seen one brought to the gaff despite some very skilled attempts to do so. And it was no different this time. After a minute of two, it parts away and a new set of gear has to be bent on.

By now the light is going out of the water and the mackerel are starting to go off the feed.

"Well, personally, I think we have had a very good day," says our skipper. "What say you we head for home to mother?"

"Fucking good idea," comes from me and Nibblo.

"Okay then, slack the mizzen and I'll bring her around."

I clamber aft, balancing along the tops of the pound boards to get to the sheets. Bonzo goes into the wheelhouse and jams the engine into gear and winds up the throttle. The old engine belches out a huge cloud of black smoke to clear its throat after a day on tick-over before settling down clean and clear, rumbling away at a steady 900 RPM. Nibblo nips down into the cabin to put the kettle on, and there we are, tired out and homeward bound with a good catch of fish. There is no better feeling.

We approach the Banjo pier at Looe and Bonzo winds back on the throttle to enter the harbour at a respectable speed. Then, slowing down to tick over and finally knocking her out of gear, we nudge alongside the quay to get our fish ashore, but what a clamour. Thirty boats all wanting to land at once; everyone wants to get home and it is utter mayhem. On the decks of deeply laden craft, men are working flat out, hoses and buckets in action, to wash the catch. Fish are being hurriedly sorted and scooped into five stone boxes, then flung up onto the quay and stacked up onto wooden pallets. Boats that have landed are manoeuvring to let another alongside the quayside. From one end to the other the quay is twinkling with working and navigation lights, there's plenty of shouting and banter, and all to the background thrum of the diesel engine. But eventually, out of this chaos comes order, and within a couple of hours or so, all is tranquil once more and the boats are snubbing quietly at their moorings A few terns are shrieking on the river, and the only human sounds now are of the muffled voices and laughter of the packing gang (twenty or so men) inside the fish market, working long into the night to get the day's catch boxed, iced and loaded onto the lorries.

5

Prosperity

Shoals of mackerel, trillions strong, were arriving to winter off the Cornish coast. While we were making big catches in the Radar Buoy area, the Newlyn boats were loading off at the back of St Michael's Mount. But this handy to home fishing was not to last for very long, because the over-wintering area of choice for these huge shoals seemed to lay somewhere between the Western Blackhead and Dodman Point, with the biggest concentrations usually in the Falmouth bay area. It was here that the shoals sometimes packed in so densely boats could steam over them for miles on end with their echo sounders blacked out from top to bottom. Even the most experienced skippers had never witnessed anything quite like it before.

As the shoal that we had started to fish on moved west, the one in Mount's Bay came east. Both made their way to Falmouth, followed closely by the boats that had been hunting them. So effectively the whole of the Cornish mackerel fleet were focusing their efforts in the one area, all working on one immense concentration of fish.

In those days, it took the boats an average of four hours to open up St Anthony's light in Falmouth bay from Looe, bashing away against the wind that always seemed to be blowing fresh and gusty from somewhere in the westerly quarter. Rare was the morning we weren't in for a bumpy ride with plenty of flying spray, but thankfully this also gave us a fair run home which is definitely the right way around when making passage in a heavily laden boat. Having such a long steam to the fishing grounds each morning meant, tides permitting, we had a very early start to the day. By four o'clock in the morning, Looe harbour would be a rumble of activity, the muffled chat and laughter as crewmen dragged tiers of boxes from under the fish market to be stacked aboard for the coming day's fishing; the clattering mechanical roar followed by clouds of choking grey smoke as yet another well-worn engine erupted into life. Much chit chat as legs and fenders are unshipped, the sharp tinkling noise made by the quayside mooring rings when the ropes are slipped. And when the last boat burbles its way out to sea, peace and tranquillity descend again, harbour lights reflecting into glassy calm water, the only sounds the mewing of a few terns and gulls. The occupants of the cottages close to the harbour side roll over in bed and try and snatch a little more sleep; bottles rattle intermittently in their crate as a milkman does his round, door to door .

Out in Looe Bay and while still in the shelter of the island, the boats stop for a few minutes to hoist their mizzen sails. Tightly sheeted home, this sail will act like a shock absorber, easing out much of the plunge, roll and jump when steaming head to sea.

Aboard the *Prosperity* we quickly set our mizzen and then nip smartly for the shelter of the wheelhouse, closing the door behind us. It's not in the least bit inviting out there, cold, dark, wet and windy. Bonzo winds the engine into gear and proceeds to pick a way down the shallow rocky channel that runs between Looe Island and the mainland. Scrabbling at the wheelhouse door, Nibblo bursts in, pot of tea in hand, his donkey jacket and hat sparkling with beads of water. He has just run the gauntlet from the cabin hatch on the fore deck, and for his trouble he has been lashed with a cat's paw of spray.

"Well done, that's just the job," we greet him.

"All I can say is, I hope you pair appreciate the things I do for you," comes the reply.

"You're a wonderful little chap, of that there is no doubt," I parry.

"Bollocks," he retorts. "Put the light on a minute Bonz so I can see to pour the tea."

There's a click, and a begrudging yellow glow seeps around the wheelhouse, three mucky chipped mugs are pulled out from wherever they had been wedged, a slop of tea tipped into one is swilled from mug to mug and then jettisoned out of the lee window. Thus, suitably washed out, the ready-milked and sugared tea is poured into them and from the same pot through the course of a long day may well come coffee, soup or cocoa. The light is quickly switched off - the man steering must not lose his night vision. Braced against the roll and pitch of the boat we enjoy a breakfast of tea and biscuits. Nibblo hangs off the end of the first of his forty Woodbines, the smoke from which thickens up the cold damp air of the wheelhouse.

In the pitch darkness, the loom of the land can be made out on the starboard hand, black against a dark grey sky. Clearing the island channel, Bonzo puts on a bit of port wheel to clear Oarstone Point and then gives the engine full throttle; SW by W will take us clear of the Dodman Point and on down to Falmouth Bay. Polperro light is winking away on the cliffs abeam of us while over the luff of the starboard bow the distant lights of Gorran Haven and Mevagissey appear to dance in between the vicious winter squalls whirling out of Par Bay. All around us the red and green navigation lights of our fleet bob and curtsy, while their white masthead lights slice madly about in the blackness above them.

In the *Prosperity*'s wheelhouse Bonzo is perched up on the steering chair while Nibblo and I are on the bench seat aft. The only illumination is the low glimmer of the master clock on the old Mark V Decca Navigator clicking endlessly around, red, green, purple, red, green, purple, the colours in deep hypnotic shades. A tiny yellow diode glowing on the front panel of the VHF radio indicates that it is switched on, but of that we are very well aware as the air is now full of gossip from the other boats; channel eight is red hot with news of how the local pool and darts teams are fairing, an update on the health of someone's wife or mother who had recently been poorly, or just general leg-pulling and joke telling, all vital stuff. We are now starting to pick up the SW ground swell, a long lazy surge under running the messy top wash caused by the fresh nor-westerly wind now blowing. And so we plunge along, our old engine burbling away comfortably in the engine room beneath our feet. The faster boats such as the *Tethra*, *Ella* and *Ganesha* have now opened up a lead over the rest of us. These three are among the newest in the fleet and have the power to touch nine knots, while most of the others are lucky to average seven or maybe eight if you really strangle the last bit of power out of the engines, something very few skippers like to do. But those three greyhounds have not got it all their own way because the old lugger *Our Boys*, now under the ownership of two keen young fishermen, Tony and Robert Chapman, has recently had a massive refit and sports two powerful modern engines. And what a gallant sight the old girl makes, stern tucked down in the water, stem sloping back like a WWI destroyer, cutting through the fleet at a good nine knots, not bad for a craft that started life under sail and oar back in 1904.

Pencarrow Point comes abeam and we open up Lantic Bay before the lights of Fowey come clear of Punchy Cross and Gribben Head marks the start of Par Bay, a horrible stretch of water when a fresh north west wind is blowing. Waves, steep and angry, can build up over a ten mile fetch and smash against the side of the boat sending sheets of spray flying across the deck. Every now and then the boat will synchronise her rolling with the waves, and then it's hang on tight as she wallows rail to rail, the sudden and violent motion giving everything in the wheelhouse a good excuse to jump from its place and roll madly around the floor.

Leads and feathers, cups and spanners have all escaped and are going crazy. Bonzo is clinging to the wheel while Nibblo and I are trying to catch and stow the gear that has made a bid for freedom, giving the *Prosperity* a round and thorough cursing at the same time.

"Don't talk to my boat like that," says Bonzo.

"Fuck her," says Nibblo. "Look what the old cow has just done."

With order restored we plough on, the lashing spray and energy sapping motion starting to ease a bit as we battle across the bay, the lights of Mevagissey fading down behind Chapel Point and thankfully we start to gain more of a lee. Dodman Point now looms high on the starboard hand, marking the halfway point of our voyage. The fleet ploughs on at a steady six or seven knots, gaining in number as boats from the fishing villages we pass along the way join us on the dark and windy trek westward. Landmarks are mentally ticked off in a vain attempt to get away from the Dodman that seems to linger close astern forever. Verryan Bay, Gull

Rock and Gerrans Bay crawl past us in the darkness, and then St Anthony's Head, the eastern sentinel of our goal, Falmouth Bay, is abeam. Not only that, after a false dawn lasting so long you think it is never going to happen, daylight arrives, filtered meanly through low scudding winter clouds. It lifts your mood, driving away the lonely isolated feeling that darkness always gives. The towns of Mylor, St Mawes, Flushing, Penryn and Falmouth play host during the mackerel season to the boats from Padstow, Newquay, St Ives, Penberth Cove, Newlyn, Penzance, Porthlevan and Cadgwith, and what a cross section of craft there are. Twenty foot open boats from the coves of Penberth and Cadgwith, French trawlers, Scots ring netters, Devon crabbers, Cornish luggers, Thames bawlies, Newlyn long liners and every class of fishing vessel ever built in Cornwall. These boats are now pouring out past Black Rock and into the bay, and it's not long before the skippers of the lead boats are on the radio blaring out the news of solid markings on the echo sounder and jumbo mackerel up in the water. Aboard the *Prosperity* we pull on our sea boots and oilskins, Nibblo and I go out on deck to ship up the gurdies and make ready. Nothing more can be done until we join the fleet, now becoming visible as a forest of masts and black smoke on the western skyline.

6

Pilot Whales

A mile away from the main fleet the echo sounder is switched on and instantly the graph paper is blacking out from top to bottom. It hasn't suddenly developed a fault, this is solid fish and whales as well. Hundreds of pilot whales have gathered in the bay, not to hunt mackerel as they don't seem the least bit interested in them, but the squid that lie under the mackerel shoals.

Bonzo passes the wheel over to me and goes forward to his line. Nibblo fishes amidships and I work aft by the wheel house door. How I became skipper when we worked the lines I have no idea. Nothing was ever said, it just happened. Getting very close to the fleet I eased the engine back, just nudging along to get through the whales.

"Give her a try here," says Bonzo.

"Hang on a minute," I reply, "I just want to get her up by the Castle Wray, they've got them solid".

In truth every one 'had them solid' but in a fleet of boats numbering hundreds you have to start somewhere. I stop her up a couple of boat lengths astern of the St Ives long liner *Castle Wray* and away go the lines, but not very far. The top hooks are only just under the water when the downward plummet of the three pound lead is arrested, by the sheer mass of fish fighting to get on the hooks. These fish are so big and lively that you nearly need two hands to wind your gurdy up, but come up they must. An arm span at a time, the line is lifted aboard as you move backward along your working space, here and there dropping bights of line into a fish box or over a pound board to try and prevent tangles. The last fish aboard leaves the lead on its long strop hanging over the rail then, a span at a time, the fish are whacked off the line with a sharp jerk, and when all is clear down you go for more. And so we carried on, line full after line full, only stopping to clear the odd tangle or to scoop the working area clear when you could no longer move your feet. With the mizzen set, a dab ahead on the engine every couple of minutes keeps the boat up head to wind, a nice steady working platform whatever the weather.

We fish on like this until around midday, by which time the deck is like a slaughter house with blood, slime and scales thickly lagged onto everything, your hat, face, oilskin and every part of the boat. The sets of gear are worn out, and we can hardly stem our boots through the fish that lay calf deep in the working area. And hunger and thirst are overtaking us. It is high time for a clear up and a bite to eat.

Nibblo grabs the deck hose to clean off his boots and oilskin before going down forward to put the kettle on while Bonzo and I proceed to scoop the fish into boxes and deck pounds to clear the working areas. The hose is then slashed about to try and clean things up a bit, by which time Nibblo is filling the mugs with steaming hot tea. Labour now ceases for ten minutes or so while we attend to the loudly protesting inner man. Standing on deck with a mug of tea in one hand and a sandwich in the other allows time to look about, and what a scene presents itself. One that I will never forget. Hundreds of boats working a shoal of fish several miles wide, while the space between every boat is filled with pilot whales, diving and swimming or just laying on the surface looking at us. The air and sea full of birds, gulls fighting and squawking, gannets quacking loudly as they plunge after fish, skuers robbing the gulls, and guillemots in little groups quietly going about their business. It was a scene that was nothing short of spectacular, and I doubt I shall witness its like again.

When the tea mugs are drained, we cut off the old feather sets and bend on new, but on the first drop we find a much smaller grade of fish. We have drifted too far to lee, so have to steam back up to the main fleet to find the big jumbos again. The only snag is that the whales are lying around us so tightly we daren't move the boat. Nibblo goes to the bow shouting and bawling at them and banging the hull with a broom but that does no good.

"Alright," says Bonzo, "we will have a bit more of a sort out until they shift enough for us to move."

There is nothing more we can do, so for a few minutes we wash the fish and scoop them into boxes, picking out the odd small one as we go. But at last there is a gap in the whales and we are able to move ahead.

"Aye, aye Captain," says Bonzo. "Put her in gear, but for Christ's sake don't hit one, he'd sink us."

At no more than three knots I con the *Prosperity* back to the fleet and we resume our fishing. The lines are released, back line playing through the right hand, the fingers of the left tap tapping on the arms of the spinning gurdy to prevent override, the lead plunging away down through millions of voracious fish darting like missiles at the lured hooks dragged behind it. A quick jig on the line to make sure all the hooks are taken, and then up they come. As the top swivel of the line breaks clear of the water, frenzied mackerel swim the line to the surface in a desperate fight to regain their liberty. As the afternoon wears on, all the pounds and boxes are brimming with mackerel and we are each struggling to work with so many fish laying on the deck. It can't be very far away from home time, and as if to corroborate this thought, billows of black smoke are to be seen here and there around the fleet indicating some of the boats are already underway.

"Here, Ned," says Nibblo, observing this. "What's the time by the wheelhouse clock?"

I glance in the door: "Three o'clock," I reply.

"Bonze," he says. "It's going to be late enough time we steam home and land this lot."

Bonzo looks up from his line. "It's not often I agree with you Nibblo, but this time I do. Up lines, it's time to head for the hills."

Up come the lines and the last fish of the day are shaken off and the worn out sets of gear are cut from the swivel. Gurdies are unclamped from the rail to be stowed down in the fish room. Next we hose each other down with the deck wash and broom to remove the thick coating of slime, blood and scales clinging heavily to our boots and oilskins. That done, the skipper comes aft to steer, down goes the wheel and the engine throws up a huge plume of smoke as he winds on the throttle.

"Sheet away the mizzen," he shouts, and we are soon around on course for home.

By now nearly all the boats are under way; those from Falmouth will be in and landing within an hour, but the Looe boats have furthest of all to go. It will be eight o'clock or more before we can take our oilskins off.

Apart from a ten minute break at lunch time we had been hard at it since just after dawn, and now the thing we all need is a sit down, a mug of tea and a bite to eat. Nibblo appears with a pot of tea and for twenty minutes or so we enjoy a well-earned break. But all too soon, Nibblo tosses his fag end out of the open door of the wheelhouse and stands up.

"Come on then, Ned." he says. "We've got a lot of work to do before we can land this lot."

Bonzo turns around from his steering. "How many do you reckon we've got?" he asks.

Between the three of us we tally over the pounds and boxes and agree that it must be around six hundred stone, a very good day's work. Mind you, if we have got six hundred then some of the hard driving four handed boats will probably have well over a thousand stone. Daylight is fading so the deck lights are switched on as Nibblo and I hobble stiffly out on deck to start washing and grading the fish. Mackerel are put into three grades, large, medium and small, but because this catch is basically all large, the grading won't take too long. It's a big catch so we have no spare boxes. Instead a box is emptied on to the deck and hosed out clean, then another box of fish is hosed and tipped into the first one, picking out the odd medium or small as we go, and so on. When the boxes are all sorted and stacked, we start on the pounds. First a pound is cleared of its fish and hosed out, then it's refilled, a scoopful at a time, picking and sorting as we go, the deck wash playing on them meanwhile. By the time the last pound is sorted we are abeam of Polperro; half an hour to go to Looe, and just time for a final pot of tea.

Steaming into harbour, the usual mayhem awaits us. A hundred tired and hungry men just wanting to put their catch ashore, moor the boat up and get home for dinner and some kip. The noise: engines revving and thrumming, the metallic quaking of VHF radios, the shouting, laughter and banter of voices, mooring chains tinkling, the scraping sound of boxes being dragged along the quay, a sharp crack as a pallet is dropped in place and the rumble of heavily laden pallet trucks as a packers pull the swaying load up to the market. And of course the gulls! Shitting, squawking, fighting and robbing fish wherever and whenever an opportunity presents itself. We join this chaos, slamming the pallets, dragging the boxes and swearing at the gulls and by half past eight the three of us are stood on the quay ready to go home, the catch put ashore, the boat moored up snugly and all scrubbed down.

"Fuck it," says Nibblo. "I think I've had enough for one day." And so say all of us.

7

Heavy Weather

High pressure dominated the weather system over the south west for the next few days, giving the fleet the blessing of some calm clear days and enabling it to work some very long hours hauling deck loads of jumbo mackerel aboard off Falmouth. Make the most of it, we said to ourselves, conditions like this won't hold for long in winter time and, of course, they didn't.

On our third day out the weather was forecast to change. A massive low pressure system was working its way in from the Atlantic and radio broadcasts had been interrupted to issue gale warnings for Portland, Plymouth, Lundy, Fastnet and Irish Sea: south west, force five to seven, perhaps gale eight later. But as a light breeze was still blowing off the land and as the tide would be ebbing for most of the day, we were fairly confidant of coming home with yet another good catch before it hit us. That's if it did. Among fishermen, weather forecasters are not held in very high regard. Skippers will bear a forecast in mind, but make their own decisions about the weather conditions, with many of the harder men working hours into a rising gale to win a day's pay. They were not reckless in their actions, never running to lee to look for fish on a poor forecast, always to weather when, if it did come on to blow, they would have a fair run home.

And so, in the darkness of a calm winter's morning, the Looe boats ploughed their watery furrows down to Falmouth bay, joined en route by others from Polperro, Fowey and Mevagissey. We met the rest of the Cornish fleet halfway between St Anthony's Head and the Manacles reef where they lay with their echo sounders blacked out quietly awaiting the dawn while drifting over a massive shoal of fish. And when at last daylight did creep down into the tarry black depths we released our lines, to be rewarded instantly with a magnificent jumbo mackerel on every hook, fighting and glittering, green, blue and silver as we toiled hour after hour to haul seemingly endless strings of them over the rail, to expire on the deck, a mass of blood, scales and machine gun bursts of beating tails.

As we fished, an oily ground swell started to work its way into the bay from the south west and the sun, shining like a disc of cheap lacquered brass, climbed up into a powder blue sky. By late morning the coming bad weather was starting to show its hand, the boats now with their bows pointing to the south west from where irritable little draughts of wind began to ruffle the surface of the sea. The western sky brooded and sulked , as angry looking clouds billowed and rolled, while low along the southern horizon 'post boys', puffy little white clouds, broadcast their warning as did the tiny chunk of rainbow alongside the sun, aptly called a sun dog. Nature was writing its storm warnings up in the sky, loud and clear. At midday we stopped for our usual quick bite to eat and to clear the deck up a bit. This also gave us a chance to look around.

Bonzo glanced to the west, to the south and up at the sun, then carried on scooping fish into boxes. Nibblo carried the pot of tea aft to the wheelhouse and we trooped in after him.

"Have you pair seen that lot up in the sky?" he said.

"I know what our father would say if he was here now," replied Bonzo.

"Yes," said Nibblo. "Fuck off a bit quick."

But to drive fishermen off good fishing takes more than the threat of bad weather, so the last bite of sandwich was swallowed down with a mouthful of tea and back to the lines we went. On and on we worked, hardly looking left or right, brains in neutral. I dabbed the engine in and out of gear to keep the lines up and down in the water to prevent us from driving back out of the shoal of the fish and lessen the chances of fouling the lines up. But by now the breeze was increasing and the engine was in gear more often as the bow heaved up and down in the oncoming swell. We were all aware that this would probably be the last chance to earn any money for several days. The fish were of the right sort, big ravenous and easy to catch, right up in the water, so all the boats fished on.

By now some of the smaller open boats were starting to look well down in the water, but still they rode to the seas and carried on fishing. Eventually the twenty foot cove boats peeled away from the fleet and got underway for home, heavily laden as they surfed in towards Falmouth, rail deep in foam. Two men on a plank, we called them, tiller steered and open to all the weather, the only bit of comfort aboard was a flask of tea. Theirs was the toughest call of all.

By now it was not looking very good at all. The wind was a good force five and signs in the sky were telling us the bellows would soon be blowing much harder. Everyone had got a good day's work aboard, but still most were tempted to stay on just that bit longer; none of the bigger boats wanted to be seen getting under way at the same time as the little cove boats. The engine was hardly out of gear now, the old gearbox grinding away as we stemmed into the cresting and breaking seas, the gurdies whirling around like little windmills as ever more fish were pulled aboard. The VHF radio came to life as a few of the boats got under way.

"We've just had a beauty sea smash aboard, washed everything around, the crew are digging out on the pump. I am going to take that as a sign to get underway," said one skipper.

"Aye aye, skipper, we are in along with you. We're loaded deep enough for this weather, that's for sure," came his mate's reply. And so the day's fishing began to draw to a close as boat after boat peeled away from the main fleet and headed for home. The wind was now a good force six/seven and the seas were steep and building, cresting and breaking. It promised to be a lively ride back up the coast.

Aboard the *Prosperity* I gave a wave to the Looe boat *Paula* as she surfed past us heading up towards the Dodman.

"Here, do you pair think we've got enough aboard, or what?" I ask.

"What's up with you, Ned, got the water in or something?" shouts Nibblo as he thrashes another lineful of mackerel down on the deck.

"Water in be fucked," I reply. "If we don't get under way soon we'll be lucky if we don't get half the fish swept off the deck as we bring her around."

"My line is about fucked and I'm not going to bend on a new one this time of day," chips in Bonzo.

"Look here," retorts Nibblo. "The Our Daddy is still fishing, and I am buggered if we are going to get underway before her."

So nothing more is said and we fish on. By now the engine is continually in gear; in fact I have put the throttle on a bit to keep her driving up into the weather.

After another ten minutes or so Bonzo looks up: "It's high time we got underway. If you want to stay on, Nibblo, I'll launch the life raft and you can float around for the night in that."

"'Ark to that little bastard," says Nibblo to me, a look of wounded pride on his face. "Trying to make the best of the day, and that's all the thanks I get."

"It's fuck all to do with that," retorts Bonzo. "All you're worried about was the Our Daddy. Anyway she's just coming around now, so if you really don't mind we'll do the same."

"Do what you like, you miserable little fucker," Nibblo glares back. "I'm going down to put the kettle on." And with that, he hoses off his oilskin and flounces off down the cabin.

"Whatever can you do with a little twat like that?" says Bonzo to me.

"It looks like you've upset him again," I reply, trying to stay as neutral as possible. He and I hose the muck off our own oilskins and boots

"Righto, Captain," says Bonzo. "Stand by the mizzen sheets. I'll pick the moment to bring her around."

We ride head to for a minute or so and then, rearing up over a great lump of a sea, we swoop down the other side. Our moment has arrived, down goes the wheel and on goes the throttle.

"Slack away the sheet," yells my little ginger captain and so, to a fanfare of engine roar and a plume of black smoke, the *Prosperity* comes about, putting her stern to the weather as clean as you like, no waves breaking over us and nothing rolling off the deck. Now we are running before the weather and it feels like a different world, the sting goes out of the wind and the seas don't seem half as menacing. Although we are surfing along on some real monsters at times, with a good boat under our feet and a good man at the helm the trip was, in an odd way, a pleasure and not a danger.

Nibblo bursts into the wheelhouse, pot of tea in hand, looking like he had just come around Cape Horn with it.

"Fucking glad I'm not on one of the open boats," he exclaims. "It's fairly piping out there now."

"It won't be much fun on one of them right now," I join in.

Bonzo turns from the wheel to take his mug of tea: "Did you see the state of the Ella and Ganisha?" he exclaims. "Loaded right down in weather like this, and the greedy bastards were still fishing when we left… Look out boys, here's a big one!"

The old boat is now tearing along on the crest of a huge breaking sea, the deck awash in foam and the engine governor going crazy because the boat is going faster than the engine can rev. The sea then overtakes us and we slide down its back into the trough behind, only to be picked up by another one not much smaller than the first.

"We shall be home in record time tonight," I say, listening to the governor trying to control the engine. Voices crackle over the VHF, telling us that all the boats are now heading homeward. Some of the heavily laden open boats are shipping a drop of water, and there is a fair bit of pumping going on to keep them free, but providing none of their pumps choke up they will be okay. Let's hope that God has got them all under his wing tonight.

After a bite to eat, Nibblo and I go out on deck on hands and knees to try and sort out some of the pounds of fish. This we partially succeed in doing, but it is dreadfully hard work in such conditions, and eventually we say fuck it and crawl back into the wheelhouse to finish the job later, back in harbour.

To enter the peace and safety of the harbour from the boiling breaking seas of a winter's gale is a truly wonderful feeling. On the *Prosperity*, a forty foot, fully-decked boat, we were in no real danger unless something went badly wrong, but many of the working fleet at that time were 25 to 38 feet length of hull with an open hatch board deck in the working area, and any seas breaking aboard had to be pumped out. A few were of recent construction, packing plenty of power for their day, with both hand and engine operated bilge pumps. But many of the fleet were getting on in years, most of them very under powered and possibly with only one hand pump to keep them free. Plus some pretty ancient luggers were still in commission, fine old sea boats with a track record second to none, but when it came to a real good hammering the crew could be as busy on the pump as the men on the open boats. Being caught out in a breeze was something that had to be accepted if you went commercial fishing for a living, although in a well found craft the dangers were not great providing everything does what it is supposed to do. It's when the unexpected happens, like a pump choking up, or the engine stopping, whatever it may be. In fine weather it's not hard to clear the pump or find out what is wrong with the engine. But in bad weather everything is ten times harder to achieve, and if a tow home is needed, then there can be some very big problems for all concerned. In a gale of wind you can go from all's well to a potentially life threatening situation in the blink of an eye. Upon arriving safely in harbour after such an event the first thing you want to know is who has yet to make it in. And nobody will rest until the last boat is safely home.

One by one, the heavily laden boats make it back into port, many of them still pumping as they steam in, with both men and boats looking battered and weary, well reflecting what they have just been through. When such a gale blows you arrive home feeling exhausted, but the likelihood of conditions being fit to go to sea the next day are minimal, so there is usually the chance of a good night's kip to recover. A few jobs would need to be done on the boat the next morning, tip diesel, scrub down and do the usual running repairs that keep a wooden boat seaworthy. After that, a pint in the pub before lunch where, around the fire, tales of the previous day's heroics would be recounted while smocks and overalls turn white as the salt in them dries out, causing fish scales to shed onto the floor and tables like a miniature snowstorm. The favourite pub was the Salutation in East Looe, and when the place was full of fishermen the scale problem was so great that the landlord, George Rider, would detail a barmaid to go around with a dustpan and brush sweeping up. The bar, the floor and all the tables would be smothered in mackerel scales. I remember apologising once for the mess, to which George replied that it would be a very poor time for all concerned when there were no scales to sweep up. How very prophetic that statement proved to be.

8

Searching

A winter gale might be over and gone in twenty four hours. There again, it might last a week, or a really bad spell of weather could set in making it impossible to go to sea for a month. You never knew; life as a fisherman is a complete lottery. There are good times when you think you will never be poor again, and times when the boats are double roped and fendered alongside the quay as the storms run up through the Channel one after the other. Meanwhile, the bit of money that you managed to put by in the good times is draining fast away, while at the same time bills, for the moment totally un-payable, pile up on the mantelpiece. It is then that you seriously doubt the wisdom of the life, but when the sun shines again and you can once more enjoy the freedom to range the Channel hunting the mackerel shoals, then bad times are soon forgotten and you wouldn't swap your way of life with anyone.

Leaving port in the darkness of a fine morning after the gales have passed, I watch the sun rising in the south east and claw its way low into the sky, there to blind you all day long as it carves an arc just above the southern horizon. Both sea and sky are pale indigo in colour, while the boats rise and fall on the ground swell running on an otherwise calm sea.

Where the shoals of mackerel might be found nobody could tell. After a period of very turbulent weather the fish will seek sanctuary in deep water. But the search for them will be conducted from Bigbury Bay, east of Plymouth, to the Runnelstone buoy down near Lands End. Three hundred boats will be combing the Channel with their echo sounders, so someone will find them sooner or later. But until the big shoals settle back in Falmouth bay or wherever, and everyone knows once again where to head for, we are all playing a guessing game. The boats that found the fish would load off, and

43

those within a reasonable steaming distance would make a day's work. But others too far away would go home empty and content themselves with the knowledge that they know in which direction to head the next day.

There was a sly method of avoiding the big search and this was practised by a few crafty skippers, enabling them to land a modest catch, burn very little diesel and then benefit the next day from those who had been out looking. There is an area off Whitsand bay known as the 'mud', and here a small stock of jumbo mackerel lived. The same sort of thing could be found off Plymouth Sound, tiny marks on the sounder would render a couple of lines-full and with patience a hundred stone or so of quality fish could be landed at the end of the day. There was nothing wrong with that, except that these sly characters would be the first away the next day, once they knew where the big shoals had been located. Take all and risk nothing was their motto.

A week of storms eventually passed up through the Channel before the boats were able to get back to sea. On the first day out, the *Prosperity* was headed out to the SSW, a course that took us out to the Radar buoy ground, a fairly fishy area, but it was also middle ground and gave us a fighting chance both east and west if a scry went up.

All was made ready for action, the gurdies were clamped on the rail, each one sporting a brand new set of feathers; channel eight on the VHF was jammed with traffic but it was all the usual old bollocks: pool, darts, news and gossip. By dawn light we were out at the Radar buoy, the echo sounder was switched on and the hunt commenced. And it was all eyes about, for there was much to look out for, such as gannets diving, other boats suddenly coming around, marks on the echo sounder or a shout on the VHF. Everyone was wound up like a clock spring hoping that when the scry went up it was us that found it, or at least whoever did was within reasonable steaming distance of us. But this particular day that had started with high hopes led on to frustration and finally, as the fruitless hours rolled on, boredom and indifference. It was a syndrome known as 'Red hot meter and empty tanks'. Hundreds of boats steaming hundreds of miles and nothing worthwhile was found, just a few small marks on the meter resulting in a few lines full of immature fish. The winter storms had driven the mackerel shoals well off the coast and we just had to be patient and wait until they reappeared. So we arrived back in harbour late in the afternoon with a few boxes of small stuff that wouldn't pay for the tea bags we had used, let alone the diesel that had been burnt. Fishermen live all their lives with the great uncertainty; it would all come good another day, but today was not to be that day.

And come good again it did. Over the winter season we chased the mackerel shoals from Bigbury Bay to the Lizard for big catches and small on days when the sea sparkled calm in the sunshine and other days so horrible you wouldn't wish the misery of it on condemned prisoners.

By early March the hand line season was all but over. The fish were migrating from the coast, leaving just a few harum-scarum shoals here and there, and they were hardly worth the effort of hunting down. Everyone who had taken part in the hand line fishery had earned good wages, and now many of the boats would simply mark time until the paint up in May and the commencement of the summer pleasure angling. By the time the older wooden boats had finished a winter's fishing there was no denying they were in very desperate need of some TLC. Many would be showing their plank seams from stem to stern through hard driving while heavily laden in poor weather, or when the Atlantic ground swells were running high they had motored to the top of a big sea only to find the next one missing, the crew, wide eyed and white knuckled, brace themselves as the boat plummets with a tooth shattering crash down into a deep watery pit. For a split second the air in the cabin and wheelhouse is full of flying objects as leads and spanners, tea mugs and sets of feathers are propelled from their stowage, while on deck pound boards unship, letting boxes of fish capsize. The boat has gone from order to utter crashing rolling mayhem in about two seconds. The fight is on to get back up head to wind and regain control because the next wave may well break foaming over her and as a boat can't float on foam she gets buried in it, to be left wallowing like a half tide rock. It's then 'pump, boys, pump' because one more like that and it's goodnight Vienna. It was really not surprising that the poor old boats looked a bit forlorn come spring. The deck wash and broom, the fish scoop, boxes, fish and lines all conspired to strip the boats back to bare wood. Add to this a leak or two in the hull and there's the full picture of how a mackerel boat may well look at the closing of the winter season. Not a pretty sight, but nothing that a good paint up and refit couldn't cure.

9

Trawling

To bridge the gap between the end of the mackerel season and the spring paint up, the *Prosperity*'s crew would wind on the trawling gear. Two boats, the *Tethera*, skipper Ivan Chaston, and the *Anne Louise* (formerly *One Accord*), skipper Charlie Jaycock, trawled full time, while two or three others like the *Prosperity* used it as a useful stopgap between seasons. Today Looe has been a trawling port for many years, but back then it was a new trade and there was much to learn. Bonzo did fit the boat out with good trawling equipment later on, but at the time I am writing about it was all a bit of a lash up.

The gantry that took the hanging blocks and trawl doors was fabricated out of scaffold poles, the hydraulic winch had come off a much smaller boat and was never man enough for the job. We had to jump up and down on the bridles to get it to haul the last few fathoms aboard; that's if it didn't blow a hydraulic pipe, a not uncommon occurrence when hauling with a big swell running. Below decks, rolling and slipping around in spilled hydraulic oil, brandishing a well worn pair of Stilsons, trying to change pipes was not a lot of fun. Another thing we had to be a bit wary of was the warps jumping out of their lead blocks. These Bonzo had utilised from open sided guide wheels from her seining days in Scotland. A shackle catching in them at the wrong angle would result in them jumping out and flying across the deck in fine style. It's a wonder nobody was fired over board or had their head cut off.

All the paraphernalia of mackerel fishing was carried ashore and stored away, to be replaced by all the gear for trawling. A new set of wire warps was stretched down the quay to be measured and marked, then wound on to the winch, while combination spans and bridles were fathomed out and spliced up. The otter boards were slung on their chains on either side of the gantry and the starboard waterways became a net pound in which we stowed two trawls: one a wing trawl, to catch whiting, squid, monk etc, and a ground trawl for flat fish, such as lemon sole and plaice.

For our first day out with the trawl, Bonzo decided to stick to a safe bit of inshore ground known as the 'Edges' which ran up and down the shore just to seaward of the coastal rocks between Whitsand Bay and Fowey, a handy place to trial everything out. Having toiled long and hard to get the boat ready we now had to mark time for a couple of days to let a spell of blowy weather pass over, and pass it did. On the third day the weather was perfect. Bonzo laid the *Prosperity* broadside to a chilly NW wind just as dawn was clawing its way up over the eastern horizon. Nibblo and I shot the trawl away, first the thick braided net of the cod end, then one each side on the seam ropes. We paid away the much lighter net of the lengthener, then the back and belly net and finally the foot rope, wound in its chain, and the head rope with its orange plastic floats. This was all pulled out clear from the side of the boat as she drifted on the wind. Going ahead on the engine, the trawl and spans were then towed out taught astern of us from the hanging blocks in the gantry. With everything clear and looking good, the brakes on the winch were slackened off and away went the bridles, thirty fathoms of thirty mil combination. Next came the flat shackles. I am aft and clip on the doors then unchain them from the gantry. Going ahead on the engine, the starboard brake on the winch is released and the door hits the water with a splash; warp is paid out to the ten fathom mark, and the brake is wound on again. The door takes up its position and pulls down and out to starboard. All is well. Bonzo at the wheel gives a nod to Nibblo on the winch, who drops away the port door to the same effect. A plume of smoke now erupts from the funnel as the engine is wound up to a furious 750 RPM. Nibblo releases the winch brakes and with just enough tension on them to keep the gear taught, the rest of the warps are shot away out to the towing marks just shy of the bitter end. These are formed from coloured twine wound in to the lay of the warp to a length of six inches or so. At these marks the chain stoppers are wound on and the heavy rope towing bridles hooked in; the winch brakes are gently slacked away to let the bridles, made fast to the mizzen mast six foot off the deck, take the strain. Towing from a central point makes it much easier to steer. With the warps over the stern well spread and level, things are looking OK so unless a door falls over, or we come fast on a hitch, we shall tow along to give the trawl three hours fishing time before winching it back in to find out how well it has been performing. It might take a several drags to get everything adjusted and working properly, but this is where we begin.

Bonzo takes the first watch, tracking our progress on the Decca navigator as we wander down over the ground. With the tide up our arse, we are making about two knots. The time is passed drinking tea, and yarning until we are ready to engage the the clutches on the winch, the engine is eased down and the warps are wound back on to the drums. The doors break surface and are chained to the gantry before being unclipped to allow the bridles to be hauled. The poor old winch grunts and complains by the time the wing ends of the trawl reach the rail. The rest of the operation is done by hand; the foot rope is pulled aboard followed by the head rope, then as we lay broadside to weather, the trawl is hauled aboard hand over hand on the seam ropes. Hang on tight as she rolls back on a sea, and haul in the slack as she drops back again. The net narrows back like a funnel until the cod end is reached, the very last section where the fish will be. To get this aboard, a stout rope strop is wound around the net and a lifting tackle hanging from a derrick, known as a gilson, is hooked in. The tail of this is led through a lead block in the deck to the whipping drum on the winch, and the catch is hoisted aboard and lowered to just above the deck. One man reaches under the bulging net and pulls the slip knot on the cod end rope, releasing a small avalanche of trapped fish out on to the deck.

The trawl had been working well. In fact, for a first drag it was very good, five or six boxes of fine big Channel whiting, several nice monkfish, some plaice, a few cod, hake and squid. With two more drags to go, we should make a decent day's pay if the buyers don't rob us on tomorrow's market. While I retied the cod end, Bonzo has a quick look at the steel shoeing on the bottom of the doors to make sure the shine on them shows that they were down on the sea bed evenly, then the gear is quickly shot away again. Nothing builds enthusiasm like a bit of success. With the warps once more out, taught and fair under our stern, we get down on hands and knees to sort out the catch, all the different species boxed up, one from the other. All the rubbish, weed, shell, crabs and small fish etc. are shovelled overboard; the gutting knives are sharpened up and then, in the company of a million screaming squawking gulls, the catch is gutted, washed and graded. An hour sees the job done and everything washed down clean and neat; then a break for a pot of tea and a bite to eat before it's time to haul again. The trawl looks to be working well, putting us all in a good mood, so just maybe Bonzo and Nibblo won't start arguing, but it's something that you would never put money on; the slightest thing can set them off. And sure enough, in conversation Bonzo can't resist the temptation to needle his brother, and Nibblo has no more sense than to bite on the bait and away they go, hammer and tongs, shouting, swearing, turning purple and leaping up and down in absolute fury. Nibblo ends it by storming out of the wheelhouse and going down the cabin.

"There," says Bonzo, turning to me. "What do you make of that little fucker?"

"Well," I reply. "You know he bites, and you just can't resist winding him up".

"I know," responds Bonzo with a chuckle. "He makes such good sport, and I always reckon it helps to keep the blood circulating".

"While Nibblo is peaceable," I said, "you should leave him alone. It's cruel to upset someone for the sport of it."

Bonzo grins down from the wheelhouse chair, blue eyes sparkling, ginger hair bristling from under his hat. "Right then, captain," he says. "We had better see if we can sweeten him up again. Go down forward and make another pot of tea to coax him out of his bunk, and I will make sure I don't upset him".

Here I go, peace-making between the little pair again. In the cabin I fill the kettle and put it on the stove to boil. Right up in the bow, Nibblo is in his bunk, buried in blankets, only his nose is visible. I swill the teapot out and throw in a few tea bags, then sit down on the cabin locker to await the water to boil, braced against that easy roll a trawler develops in fine weather, ears cocked the while to the reassuring background rumble of the old Gardner engine as it tirelessly thrashes the prop around. After a few moments silence I hear the expected lines from the injured party.

"What do think about that little short-arsed ginger bastard? There was no need for him to carry on like that."

"I know," I reply, "I told him I thought he was a bit out of order. Anyway I am making a nice pot of tea. Are you coming up for one before we haul again?"

"Yes, alright Ned, I'll be up in a minute," he answers.

A screeching noise erupts from the kettle. Switching off the gas, I tip its bubbling contents into the pot, milk and sugar are stirred in and aft to the wheelhouse I go. As I fill up the mugs Nibblo joins us, flouncing in and not saying a word. Bonzo offers an olive branch.

"You alright now, Nibblo?" he enquires.

"Alright be fucked," comes the retort. "I was speaking to Ned down the cabin just now and he reckons you're a little cunt as well!"

Jesus wept, I think, now we are all going to be fighting. "Nibblo, I said no such thing, and you know it," I bellow. "Now, for fuck's sake, pack it in the pair of you. That's enough shouting and bawling for one day."

It does the trick. Our tea is drank in sulky silence. Bonzo glances up at the clock. "It's time to haul again," he grunts.

Thankfully, by the time we nose our way into the harbour to land our catch that evening, all the day's fighting has been forgotten. Peace on the *Prosperity* was always a fragile thing; many is the time after we had landed our catch Nibblo would tie his oilskin and sea boots up in a neat bundle and step ashore with them, swearing that he would never go to sea with his brother again. But nevertheless he was always there on time the next morning, and nothing more was said. They were two of the feistiest little buggers that I ever went to sea with. When we were mackerel fishing, many is the time we have been hauling strings of big fish aboard and an argument has kicked off, resulting in them both belaying up their lines to stand foursquare to one another, nose to nose, shouting loudly, with steam blowing out of their ears, fearlessly brandishing the waggly finger. But, for as much as they fought each other, they were intensely loyal and would have stood shoulder to shoulder to fight off the whole world if they considered that family or friends were in need of their help.

10

The Edges

The ground we called 'Edges' was always good for a day's work with the trawl. A good mix of fish could nearly always be caught there, but greater rewards were very often to be had by venturing further off.

Around the end of February the lemon-soles would appear, first up off Plymouth Sound on a big area of trawling ground known as 'Sleepy Valley' and then, after a week or so, they would work down and out into the Channel and by May they would be gone. This was clean, easy fishing and the soles could make good money on the market, so a close eye was always kept on the Plymouth boats who spent much of their time up that way. And when word filtered through that they were catching a few stone of lemons, it was time for us to shackle on the ground trawl and get up there and have a go. Working the Plymouth ground was fine, easy trawling. Apart from two well charted wrecks, there was nothing to come fast on or do any damage to the gear, hence its name. The only danger was the chance of fouling the gear of another boat because in the morning the Plymouth boats would be at the eastern end of the ground towing west, while the Looe boats would be at the western end towing east and we would all meet in the middle. This daily fleet manoeuvre called for much skilful judgment and cooperation via the VHF. Usually we all got away with it, but now and again there were a few memorable, not to say monumental, cock ups. Trawl doors dragged through a trawl, cutting it to ribbons; two lots of gear locked together and everything cable-laid. It could be enough sometimes to make you want to sell the boat and buy a farm.

Looe is an unhandy port to work from over the neap tides. You often can't get in harbour until late at night, and you have to be away again in the very early hours so, rather than go through all that rigmarole, several of the Looe boats would work out of Plymouth until the tides eased a bit.

It was pleasant easy work. You could enter and leave Sutton Pool at whatever time suited you, there was no tide to have to consider, plus, to me it always seemed like a little holiday to work from another port for a few days. We would nudge into the landing steps at the Barbican quay each evening to get our catch ashore, and when it was weighed, tallied and stowed into the fridge, the boat would be moored up for the night alongside one of the Plymouth trawlers. The next move was to get spruced up for a bit of a run ashore; oilskins and sea boots were taken off (that was a relief in itself), then to try and make ourselves a little more presentable, a bowl of hot water was shared at the galley sink to scrub the bulk of the slime, scales and general blackness off hands and faces. Overalls and smocks were removed and a comb pulled through the hair (mind you, we could never quite get rid of that just removed the hat look). And now the evening was ours: first a meal would be enjoyed in one of the little cafes or restaurants around the Barbican, apologising for the smell of fish and diesel that always entered with us (thankfully nobody seemed to mind, or if they did they were very polite about it). After a good dinner had been stowed under our belts it was time to consider a nightcap; for this the Dolphin was always favourite, a fine old pub that was situated right opposite the fish market.

Sitting around the fire with a decent pint to round off a very long day was always a great pleasure, as was the company. Old fishermen recalling the times they spent on the sailing smacks, steam trawlers and drifters; the landlady might be playing her accordion for a bit of singing and dancing, gangs of matlots or students out on the razzle would wander in, as might one or two ladies of the night, in their outrageous outfits and trowelled-on make-up.

After a couple of drinks our bunks would be calling, so after saying good night to the landlady and the old men we had been yarning with, the three of us would make our way back aboard the *Prosperity*. A quick last minute piddle over the rail, then to slip below into the warmth of the cabin, kick off our shoes and climb in our bunks, snug warm and comfortable, we would be asleep within minutes. And as the old saying goes: "You wouldn't call the King your uncle".

But no sooner had your head hit the pillow than the alarm was ringing. It's five o'clock and another day lay ahead of us. Bleary-eyed and tousle-haired, we scramble out of the bunks, pulling on overalls, smocks and sea boots. The first one togged up would put the kettle on for a pot of tea. Nibblo would then nip up to the baker's somewhere up Southside street to get some pies and cakes as grub for the day.

Bonzo would disappear down into the engine room to check everything over before firing up the engine. When cold, the old L3 Gardner could wipe out Sutton Pool in smoke; in fact, on a still morning if two or three trawlers fired up at the same time you couldn't see a boat's length anywhere. I would check over the cod end of the trawl, and then shorten up the ropes ready to cast off.

In the cold darkness of a winter's morning the boats would pass Mount Batten Pier, then head south-west to pick up the western end of the breakwater and after that, due south out to the trawling grounds, passing Picklecombe Fort, Cawsand and Penlee Point marking the end of the sheltered water. After that, if there was a fresh wind blowing the boat would start to plunge about and throw back the spray.

As the light of a winter's day was being dragged grey and unwilling up over the eastern horizon, we lay broadside to a freshening westerly wind and shot the trawl away. The doors splashed, the winch and guide blocks whirled and squealed as the boat bashed ahead on full throttle to drag out the warps and keep everything tight. Drenching cat's paws of spray lash across deck, we were all humped up like hunchbacks in our oilskins, hoods pulled down low, trying to keep warm and dry. Another day of the glorious uncertainty that is fishing had begun.

"Fuck me, it's cold and wet out there," says Nibblo as he bursts in through the wheelhouse door bearing our second pot of tea for the morning. Bonzo is perched up on the wheelhouse seat steering along a tow, the navigator clicking and flashing up its lights: red, green and purple.

"What have you bought us to eat today?" he enquires.

"Well, there is a big fruit cake, a bag of doughnuts and steak and kidney pies," his brother replies.

"We shan't starve today," says Bonzo as a large slice of cake is served as breakfast, and we chat, laugh and spin a few yarns to pass the three hours of the first watch. Then it's out on deck in the wet and the cold, braced against the relentless rolling and pitching to haul and shoot the trawl, and later gut and clean the catch. If all goes to plan we will do three drags for the day and be back in harbour and landed by about eight o'clock in the evening. We were working around fifteen hours a day and that, in commercial fishing, is not hard going.

11

Summer Season

Through the remaining winter and into early spring we earned a living with the trawl. When the weather was reasonable the boats worked what, for those days, was out deep, chasing the lemon-soles down Channel into ever rougher and more dangerous ground for the trawls and engine power that we had in those days. And if the weather was only just workable we stayed in 'Edges' after whiting, monk and plaice.

The month of May marked the end of winter. Spring had arrived and it was now time to get ready for the summer season. The *Prosperity* was stripped of all the paraphernalia of the winter fishery and taken over to West Looe for her spring paint up. And did she need it. All those old wooden boats at the end of a hard winter's fishing looked a sorry sight.

The spring paint up was a lovely time of year. If the sun shone, it would take the three of us about a fortnight of easy hours to get the old girl smart and presentable and back into her best frock for the summer visitors. At the same time I would be hauling my little motor boats out of their shed one by one and treating them to paint and varnish before re-launching them to their moorings to staunch up before putting the engines back in.

At the end of May we would all go our separate ways for the summer season: Nibblo to work his speedboat from the steps at the end of the Banjo pier doing thrill trips around the bay and pleasure trips to Fowey and Plymouth; I would be letting out my self-drive boats for trips up the river and around the bay, while Bonzo would take anglers out shark fishing in the *Prosperity*, helped by one of the local lads who wanted a holiday job. I loved the life in those days; we worked three seasons through the year and if one of these was failure for some reason, then the others would sure to be OK. We were never at anything long enough to get bored or fed up, because a new season was always just over the horizon and, what is more, compared with the ugly gnome of bureaucracy that clings parasitically to the back of every one today, we enjoyed great freedom.

I had a feeling that the summer of 1975 was going to be, shall I say, interesting, for one very good reason. Collin Mathews had put his fleet of boats up for sale and they had been purchased by Johnny Bettinson. Now Johnny was one of life's characters, about thirty years old and from an old Looe family. As a boy he had worked with his father on the motor boats before joining up and serving for ten years in the army, followed by a spell as a painter in the dockyard in Devonport. I had been working my boats for about a week before Johnny arrived on the scene. Down the river he came one morning, his boats all smartly painted and ready to go.

"Morning, Johnny," I say as I take his ropes.

"Morning, Ned," he replies as he scrambles up the ladder on to the quay. "Fuck me! What a struggle I have had to get these bastard boats ready".

"Why, what happened?" I reply.

"Well, you know what it's like leaving everything to the last minute. I was hoping to be down here yesterday but I didn't quite make it".

"What caused the delay then?" I ask.

"Well, me and the missis went out for a drink down the sports club and I made the mistake of getting involved in a round. Anyway, in the end I got that pissed I couldn't stay on my feet to get home. Sue couldn't carry me, and was going to leave me in the hedge, but as it was lashing down with rain she was afraid I would die of exposure, and she would get the blame."

This is a classic Johnny yarn unfolding here.

"Anyway, the only way she could get me to move was to beat me along with her umbrella. So there I was crawling along on me hands and knees in the pissing rain, and every time I stopped, the missis was screaming and shouting and beating the fuck out of me."

I am rolling down with laughter by this time. "How long did it take to get home then?" I enquired.

"I don't know, ages I should think. Anyway when I woke up yesterday morning not only did I have a screaming hangover but my ass and back were bruised black and blue, the knees were out of me best trousers and the toes all scratched off me best shoes, and what's more the missis is moaning because her best umbrella is all bent".

"Good start to the season then, Johnny. Do you reckon it's an omen of how the summer may pan out?" I quip.

"For fuck's sake, I hope the rest of the season doesn't match that experience," he grins.

But this is typical Johnny because only a few minutes later it is happening to him again. A few people were strolling around the quay so we start touting.

"Self- drive motor boats, lovely day for a trip up the river…" etc. Johnny gets his first let. It's a bloke and his son of about ten years old.

"Right sir," he says, "You go down the steps and I will bring the boat in to you." And with that he nips down the quay ladder to his raft of boats. He is on the third boat before he gets an engine to start, and by this time he is all worked up in a fluster, going as fast as he can to get the boat alongside and away before that engine failed as well. Clambering onto the foredeck to let a rope go, he trips on the bow cleat, emits a loud squawk and plunges headlong into the river. Now he really is in a panic, but never say die. With water pouring off him, he scrambles back aboard the boat and motors it into the steps, saying not a word to his astonished customers. His trendy bubble perm hairdo is plastered down on his head, his clothes cling to him as if vacuum-packed, and every time he takes a step, little decorative fountains of water play from his brogue pattern platform shoes. He takes their money and gives them the usual spiel about how to work the engine and where they could and couldn't go around the bay and up the river.

What the people think, I have no idea, but the whole episode is quite surreal, like something from the Goon show or the Muppets.

"Fuck me, Ned, that was my first let for the season, what's the rest of it going to be like?" And with that he squelches up to Mutton and Martin's, the clothes shop, to get a whole new rig of gear, on tick.

I worked with him for the next two summers and discovered that there was no such thing as a dull day when Johnny was about. Even his dog was mad, and its name was Crabmeat. To this day I can never work out why.

12

Looe Harbour

We were blessed with plenty of fine sunny days during that summer of 1975 and over the school holidays (the busiest period) our little motor boats were working from morning till night. It was hard work and there was always all manner of chaos going on. People, not understanding the tides, would strand their boat on a sandbank up the river or on a rock out in the bay. Nobody was ever hurt or injured, but the poor old boats took a right bashing and a long day would be extended still further by a late night expedition to retrieve a stranded boat.

The only day of the week likely to be quiet was Saturday, change-over day. People would either be arriving to start their holiday or going home at the end of it. Although we didn't earn much on a day like that, it was a blessing just to rest a bit and sit in our deck chairs drinking tea and yarning. But Charlie and Richard, the boys who worked for us, never seemed to run out of energy and would end up driving us nuts endlessly scrounging for sweets and ice creams, getting more stroppy and cheeky all the while. Eventually Johnny and I would lunge up out of our chairs at them, sending them scampering away for safety into the back streets, there to lurk about for a while keeping out of our way.

On such a day, and getting very bored myself, I was toying with the big copper petrol funnel, thinking to myself that Johnny would never fall for this old chestnut but it must be worth a try.

"Johnny," I said. "Have you ever tried the penny in the funnel trick?"

"Never heard of it," he replied.

I am in with a chance, thought I. This could be a bit of fun. "Well, get up on your hind legs a minute, I'll show you what it's about."

Adopting a very cautious manner, he hauls up out of his chair. "Oh yes, what's this all about then?"

Trying to sound as innocent and as green as possible, I say, "It's nothing, just a daft thing to pass the time, but it is not as easy as it looks".

"All right," says Johnny, "but what the fuck is it?"

"Right, I'll give you a demo. You stuff the funnel down your trousers, like so, and then put your head back and rest a coin on your forehead. Then, with eyes closed, you have to drop the coin into the funnel. It's the best of five goes, adding a coin each time you hit the target."

I could see various thoughts passing across his face as he tried to work out the catch, but in the end saw none.

"Well there's fuck all in that," he chirped.

"Tell you what, it's a lot harder than it looks," I intoned, sounding as oily as an estate agent. "I'll lay you a quid you won't get five in on the run."

Johnny cautiously takes the bait and pokes the funnel down his pants, head back with a ten pence coin on his forehead.

"Careful," I said. "Nod your head, and drop it on target." Clunk, in it goes. "Now two coins, and steady as she goes." Two coins, no problem. "Bloody hell, I'm going to lose my quid here I can see that." Johnny is chuckling and scores a bull's eye with three and four. "You lying bastard, you've done this before," I chide.

"No I haven't, honestly," he protests.

"Well, I've never seen anyone get them all in like that," I snivel. "Last go coming up, and I hope you make a balls of it."

With eyes firmly shut and five coins on his forehead he composes himself for the final drop, at the same instant I slop the funnel full, from a bucket concealed under my chair. The effect was most wonderful to behold. With eyes out on stalks, he blows his fag about fifty yards down the quay, twenty different emotions play over his face all at once as water drenches down his trouser legs onto the tarmac. "You twat, Greenwood, how the fuck did I fall for that," he howled, before convulsing into uncontrollable laughter, eyes streaming, face screwed up tight and turning a brilliant shade of purple. Way beyond being able to talk, he sort of spluttered and choked while flapping one hand around in the air. "What a gag. What a fucking gag," he was eventually able to croak. Once I get hold of a dry pair of jeans there's going to be a few bastards around here caught on that one today."

And so there was. For a couple of hours we chided passers-by who looked gullible enough to take part in the great Cornish penny in the funnel championship. In the end Claude Tamblin, who hired out boats at a set of steps further up the quay, came down to investigate. "What the hell is going on?" he questioned. "I keep hearing howls of laughter from you pair, and then some poor bugger plods up past with his trousers streaming wet."

As they old saying goes, "We hadn't laughed so much since granny caught her tits in the mangle."

* * *

Working from the harbour, the tides were always a big factor in our lives. Neap tides were fine, no big rush of water and the tide in for most of the working day, but spring tides, well, stand by for an action packed day.

The river at flood and ebb would run at about three knots. Our boats with their one and a half H.P. engines did at best about five, so the people would go hurtling up the river in fine style on the flood, but the return journey could take forever. Conversely when a boat was returning to the steps with the tide, we would signal with a big sweeping arm motion to the driver to turn into the currant, and then signal them to slow the engine right down so as to come along side in an ordered manner, and most people did just that. But every now and then a boat would come flying in on the tide, everyone aboard chatting, laughing and looking about, taking no notice what so ever of our ever more frantic signals and shouting. They would go shooting past the steps, engine still going flat out, panic then setting in, as they realise that they should now be doing something, if only they could work out what it was. Ending back out in the river again, after a few shouted instructions a second attempt would usually be more successful.

At low water we would drop the boats out into the bay and work them from a little quay called Pen Rock, at the eastern side of the beach. This always entailed plenty of anchor-work wading around in sea boots, and if there happened to be a ground swell running, you could end up wet to the waist. But it was all part of the job, and I don't think anyone would have swapped it for a job in a factory or an office.

12A

Catching A Bomb

In the mid 1970s the coastal towns and villages of Cornwall were enjoying quite prosperous times. In the prime summer months the camp sites, B&Bs, hotels and boarding houses would be full to capacity and this in turn ensured that the shops, pubs, cafés and restaurants also did a very good trade. As for the boating, the most weather dependent of all holiday activities, if the gods smiled on us then you just couldn't fail. There were more people wanting to go out boating and fishing than there were boats to take them.

Coupled with the rapid expansion of the winter mackerel fishery there was plenty of work to be had when the autumn curtains came down on the summer season. Crewing on the boats, working with the packing gangs, making up the waxed cardboard boxes that the fish were packed into, plus the many ancillary jobs and trades that kept the fleet running and, of course, the boat yards going flat out to fulfil orders for new fishing boats. A living wage could now be earned the year round, and for many people in Cornwall that was a huge bonus.

The winter of 1975/76 followed the usual pattern; huge shoals of mackerel wintering off the coast, attended by thousands of seabirds and, on occasions, an escort of scores of pilot whales. Of course, all mixed up with this was the Cornish hand line fleet, hundreds strong. On a fine calm day the fleet would drift away in the winter sunshine, working their lines over the vast shoal of fish, the crews yarning and joking boat to boat, fending off with a broom or a gaff if they got to close. Beautiful days that will never be forgotten.

Conversely there were days when the west or north west wind was blowing very fresh and every now and then we would be beaten off the deck to seek shelter in the wheelhouse as brief but extremely vicious squalls whirled off the land bearing storm force winds and hail enough to flail the skin off your face. The wind was nearly always in the westerly cant, meaning a lumpy trip down and a fine run home, but up to now none of us had thought of making use of that wind. Until one day we watched as two Mevagissey boats, the *Francis* and the *Lindy Lou*, sprout sails as they made ready for the home ward trek. I had had some sailing experience and straight away thought what a good idea. Sails would steady the boat up a fair bit, making it much easier to work on deck and maybe give us an extra knot of speed. Bonzo and Nibblo had the same thought, so on our next day in harbour we scrumped around for some canvas to fly and in the end we managed to procure two big baggy old jibs, one of which we could fly from the mizzen mast as a stay sail and the other would set from the fore masthead to the stem head. We could hardly wait to give them a try.

And we weren't disappointed for on our next run home from Falmouth bay, we had a brisk south west wind. With the mizzen sheeted away, our two extra sails trimmed and drawing well on the starboard tack, the *Prosperity* steadied right up, losing most of her old roll and wallow and, what is more, we gained a good knot in speed. This knocked about half an hour off the travelling time, putting us ahead of many of the other boats, therefore greatly reducing the immediate competition for a landing berth, boxes and pallets, which was certainly a blessing. As for the saving on diesel, well there obviously was one, but in those days it was just pennies a gallon and I can't remember it even being considered.

At one time the big shoal moved much further west and was then to be found off the Western Black Head, making the journey back and forth to Looe very much longer. As we had a good cabin on the *Prosperity* we decided to land our fish at Falmouth, it being a pleasant port to work from and made a nice change, the main attraction of course being that many hours were shorn off the working day. We landed up the river towards Penryn on what was known as Coast Lines Quay. It was one huge mackerel packing and marketing organisation, and an awful lot of boats landed their catches there. At the close of a day's fishing, rows of boats would be ranked off the quayside eight and ten deep, loaded down like half tide rocks, awaiting a turn to swing their fish ashore. When the fishing was heavy the operation just kept rolling, teams of packers

*The author (left) with 326 lbs Mako shark caught
aboard the* Guiding Star *in 1970*

Brothers Harold 'Nibblo' Butters (left) and Lewis 'Bonzo' Butters

Cousin Jack *of Penzance*

Looe mackerel boat My Lady, *skipper Alan Dingle*

Mackerel packing, Looe fish market 1970s

End of a day's trawling on Ibis *1984*

The author (right) with crewman Chris Rees, landing fish from Ibis *in Looe 1984*

Looe fish market 1980s

Crew of the Ibis *in 1981: Chris Rees (left), 'Nezzer' and the author (right)*

Mackerel boats in Looe 1980s

Ibis *racing under full sail in Looe Bay 1993*

Graham Jolliff on Polperro mackerel boat, handline with hydraulic gurdey

The author at the wheel of Ibis

Mackerel boats waiting to land their catch in Falmouth

Mike Faulkner (lost on the Claire)

'Nelson' the seal and 'Kevin' the cormorant in Looe

The author (left) with Chris Rees, landing fish from Ibis *in Looe 1984*

Ibis *entering Looe 1980s*

Mackerel catch using handline

Ibis *under sail in Looe Bay in the early 1990s*

Scots purse seiner landing catch (above)

The Ibis *bringing a Scots trawler to a halt off the Dodman (below)*

Mackerel boats fishing in fine weather

It's a hard life even on the smallest boats in the fleet

The author landing trawl fish from Ibis *in Looe*

working in shifts twenty four hours a day to clear the backlog. It was all one hell of a pantomime, but many is the time we would be landed and back down at Falmouth, ready to go ashore for a meal and a pint, while on the VHF we could hear the Looe fleet chatting away, still ploughing a furrow for home.

At Customs House Quay we would be moored with boats that hailed from ports all over Cornwall, Newquay, Padstow, St Ives and Newlyn. The bigger boats had to tie up on the outside of the quay, ranked off ten or twelve abreast, while the smaller ones would be crammed like a log jam into the little inner harbour. There were no ladders fitted to the outside wall, so to get ashore we had to scramble up a length of trawl warp that hung at each berth. But as we were all pretty fit, climbing up and down like that didn't present anything of a problem. Even Willie Bishop, a St Ives man who at the time was of pension age, if not older, could shin up the wires like a monkey.

Our evening meal was usually taken in a corner café situated just a few yards up from the quay. Fish and chips, bread and butter and a mug of tea was our favourite fare. And after dinner it was then only a short stroll to the Chain Locker for a night cap. This old pub was famous for the landlord's collection of nauticalia. Beams and walls were festooned with enough gear to fit out a clipper ship and photographs and artefacts told the story of the famous rescue of Captain Carlson and the crew of the *Flying Enterprise*, a ship rumoured to be carrying gold that foundered in the Channel during a terrible winter storm. It was a very pleasant way to bring yet another long day to a close, sat around the fire with a pint, swapping yarns with men from the other boats. Someone might lead off in song, usually the old Cornish favourites, *Little Eyes*, *Camborne Hill*, *Lamorna* etc, three part harmony on the verse and all hands roaring out the chorus. When the landlord called time, it was out again into the keen night air, all rumped up in our jackets, to yarn our way back to the welcome of the *Prosperity*'s cabin with its little black coal stove keeping it warm and snug for us. After squirting the last of the landlord's good ale over the rail, it was time for some well earned kip. A new day was beckoning, and it wasn't many hours away.

Leaving Falmouth in the morning was like joining a spring tide ebb of boats. They streamed out from everywhere: Penryn, Flushing,

Mylor and St Mawes and from moorings all up and down the river, A sharp lookout had to be maintained to keep clear of each other, although in the dark the biggest menace was Black Rock, a single unlit rock at the entrance to Carrick Roads. That thing was always a worry.

Out fishing one day, we had an incident that makes any fisherman's heart sink into his boots. Our steady, reliable old Gardner engine decided to throw a wobbler. It died down to a bare tick over, the boat fell away off the wind and we started to roll away broadside through the fleet. Bonzo immediately dived down into the engine room to find out what was ailing our trusty motor to discover that the diaphragm of the fuel lift pump had split and there wasn't a spare aboard. Here was a problem; nobody would want to stop fishing to tow us back in to Falmouth, although someone would have done just that if we had asked. The answer was to hoist the sails and see what sort of progress we could make with them. When our little bits of canvas were up and drawing, we discovered she would waddle along at about two knots and it was blowing about a five. The engine could just bear turning the prop, so at least we weren't dragging it, and the fair tide was giving us one of our two knots. But never mind, we were safe and heading in the right direction. Bonzo got on the VHF to relay our plight to the other boats, saying that we were okay but if anyone came by us, please give us a tow in. We managed to sail in to abeam of Pendennis Point and were just pondering the optimum moment to sheet home and try to make away up the river, when one of the Falmouth boats hove alongside and took our rope. Bob Harvey George was our saviour in his powerful ex-French trawler; he very soon took us up to Custom House Quay where we thankfully got our ropes ashore, glad our ordeal under sail was over. And for the cost of the petrol, Bonzo managed to organise a lift up to Looe to get the spare parts that we needed. Upon his return, an hour's work on the lift pump soon put everything back to rights.

That winter aboard the *Prosperity*, we chased the mackerel shoals from Bigbury Bay to the Lizard then, as usual, by late February their great exodus began. Where they migrated to we had no idea, but it became very much harder to make a catch. And so, to carry us through to the month of May and the spring paint up, the trawls were hauled aboard to try our luck on the lemon-sole, monk and whiting.

Trawling, if all goes according to plan, isn't usually a very exciting way to earn a living. The skipper decides where he fancies trying his luck, and this is very often based on trying to tease the truth out of the smokescreen of lies and bullshit broadcast by other skippers on the VHF the previous day. A day hauler will do three 'drags' before going in for the night, while a bigger vessel may well stay at sea for a week or more, plodding up and down the ground, day in day out, twenty four hours a day, forever adding to her catch. Working on what is called clean ground, trawling can be a steady but a very tedious way to earn a living, but it is when the skipper decides to break open some new ground that things can become much more interesting. To do this might be very rewarding, haul after haul of good prime fish, and that is why the chance is taken. But unlike the old familiar ground you don't know what is lying on the sea bed and it is then that trawling can go from days of utter boredom, to all the excitement you could possibly manage. The boat slows to a stop, the engine starts to labour and the warps come in together, the trawl has snagged on some obstacle on the sea bed, probably a rock or a piece of wreckage. The skipper might have a go at freeing it by easing back on the engine to let the boat fall back over the warps, then to put the engine flat out and charge ahead to try and drag the trawl free. This may well work and you start to move ahead again, the doors pick up and drag the warps apart and all seems okay. But at the back of your mind you are wondering if the 'fastener' has ripped the trawl and that the rest of the drag will be complete waste of time. So you either carry on, agonising in the hope that all is well, or haul to make sure that it is. It's the skipper's choice. When the trawl refuses to budge, the winch has to be engaged and the gear hauled to try and free it. If there is any tide running at the time, this operation can be quite hair-raising to say the very least. The winch grunting under the strain, the boat laying over at a crazy angle, pulled down by the warps and at the same time being swept by the tide, decks awash as she is unable to rise to the passing seas. This is a time of maximum danger; men can and do get killed and injured and trawlers can be pulled under or capsized when caught down in big tides. If the gear really won't budge then the warps are paid out again to ease the strain and the skipper will call up someone with a bigger trawler, and when it arrives the warp ends are passed over to it: then it is 'shit or bust' as the saying goes. Sometimes the trawl can be retrieved having suffered very little damage, while at other times it is hauled aboard looking as if a war party of Zulus have been through it. Occasionally the gear is never seen again, having come hard and fast into a wreck and that is that - goodnight Vienna. The warps or the combination part away and it's back to harbour for a new set of gear.

The other scenario is a weight in the trawl. The boat slows down but doesn't actually stop, the warps close in together and the engine starts to bark and black smoke with the extra strain. Once again the winch is engaged and the haul begins. The warps are wound onto the drums and the doors are chained to the gantry and unclipped. If there is something serious caught in the trawl the band will really start to play as you try to wind on the combination. The winch will be grunting and straining as it fights to bring the trawl up, inch by inch. The boat lies sluggish in the water unwilling to rise to the swell, guide and hanging blocks screech with the stress on them. At last the wing ends of the trawl appear, the brakes on the winch are wound on and you then try to get some idea of what it is that is causing all this aggro. The trawl is now hanging vertically in the water, stretched so tight that it could be made out of fencing wire. The cause could one of any number of things: fathoms of heavy steel cable abandoned by a merchant ship or a tug wrapped around the wing end, all sharp spikes and rust. A ship's anchor caught by its fluke on the foot rope, a granite boulder that has lain in wait since the last ice age lodged back in the cod end. Whatever it is, it has to be dealt with. The heaviest lifting tackle is rigged, and inch by inch the obstacle is brought to view and then is either cut away, to plunge back to the seabed, or stropped up, lifted aboard the trawler and lashed down, to be disposed of later in the trip.

By far the most unnerving of items to bring up in a trawl are old explosive devices such as bombs, depth charges, mines and torpedoes. Thousands of these things were lost or dumped at sea in the two world wars and trawlers, when exploring new grounds, would sometimes catch them. Up in the net they would come, all battered and rusty, maybe sprouting horns or fins. Some would fizz in the most alarming manner, others spewing horrible liquids and explosives from their broken casings. Even the smallest of them, if activated, was more than capable of blowing a small wooden fishing boat to kingdom come, and probably a bit further than that. Every trawler man can recall times spent struggling with these horrifying devices, crewmen refusing to help, hiding down in the cabin or right up the bow, white with fear when they realise just what sort of a gift Neptune had sent them. The skipper has to stay cool as he works out the best way to deal with the several hundred pounds of potentially instant death now in their midst. Mind you, cool as he may look, if someone were to burst a paper bag behind him he would probably jump right over the mast.

We once caught a huge bomb on the *Prosperity*. It was about eight feet long by eighteen inches wide and it was lodged right back in the cod end, so it had to be lifted aboard. The only consoling thought was that if it did detonate we wouldn't know a thing about it. We clapped a tackle on it and hauled it out of the way to spend the afternoon lashed down on the foredeck with the hose playing on it until it could be dumped over some rocky ground, and very glad we were to see it go.

There is an amusing tale of a skipper who, upon hauling a mine up in his net, got on the radio to a fellow skipper to seek his advice. Having heard the sorry tale, the advice was that there was only one course of action: "Repeat after me. Our Father which art in heaven…"

When the casings of these things rust through the explosive in them spills out and ends up rolling around the sea bed. Phosphorous will ignite when exposed to the air and water won't put it out; a dreadful substance to have aboard a boat. Other forms of high explosive may look harmless enough, but by the time the fishermen catch them they are old and likely to be very unstable. One skipper hauled up what he thought were chunks of marble and rather liking the look of it he collected it up and took it home, thinking it would make a nice decorative addition to his rockery. By all accounts it looked very well and all who saw it admired his handy work and the pretty white 'marble' glinting in amongst the alpines. Then one day a friend (who happened to be a bomb disposal expert) dropped by and when he caught sight of this rockery, he nearly had a blue fit. For there before his disbelieving eyes, were several hundred pounds of very tastefully arranged high explosive. How it hadn't gone up taking everything with it he just couldn't begin to guess. Needless to say the whole area had to be evacuated and, with all due precaution, it was removed and disposed of.

At one time, scallopers working in Falmouth bay were bringing up in their dredges what looked like clay. One skipper calling to another on the VHF enquired if he too had caught any of this 'cheesy stuff'.

"Yes," he said, "the lads are making model boats with it."

"So were my crew," came the reply. "But every time they dried out in the sun they exploded."

"Bugger me," chimed in a third, "I thought it was fire clay. I've got a lump of it home in the shed that I was going to do the Rayburn with."

But catching these things was never a joke. A scalloper working in Falmouth bay once activated a device with his dredges and, although the resulting explosion was two hundred yards or so astern of him, it collapsed his wheelhouse and shook the caulking out of the hull. No life was lost and the boat was saved, but the dredges that were on the end of his warps had vanished. But you don't always get away with it when you tangle with these things. The owners of the Brixham trawler *Twilight Waters* were becoming somewhat concerned when they couldn't contact her on the radio, so they began shouting around to other trawlers to try and get some sort of a report on her, but all to no avail. They knew the area she was working in, but none of the boats in that area could report a sighting of her. The search was then widened in case the skipper had steamed off in the night to some secret trawling ground and was maintaining radio silence because he didn't want other boats getting in on his good fishing. An 'all ships' alert was put out, but still there was no sight nor sign of the *Twilight Waters*. Where had she gone? None could say but it was starting to look very serious.

Eventually one skipper reported hearing a distant explosion during the night in the area she was known to have been in. And upon further investigation, that proved to be the clue to her fate. The verdict on the *Twilight Waters* was that she and her crew had been blown from the face of the earth when a mine or a bomb caught in the trawl had detonated as they were trying to deal with it. Nothing more than a battered life belt was ever found to bear witness to her tragic end.

Statistically speaking, commercial fishing has always been a very hazardous occupation, but add in bombs and mines and it must go right off the scale. Thankfully most of these things have long since been cleared off the main trawling grounds, but it's the men who worked there, thirty and fifty years ago, we have to thank for that.

All other mariners use their vessels to get from A to B, preferably as swiftly as possible. But not the fishermen; the sea is where they live and work, handling their boats and gear with great skill and daring, working eighteen to twenty hours a day in all weathers and conditions. And yet fishing is classed as unskilled labour. Surely, in truth, fishermen must be some of the toughest and most skilled mariners out on the water today.

14

Hot Work

It seems to me that every twenty years or so the gods that rule the elements decide that they will bless us with some really nice summer weather. This, I consider, must be as a consolation prize for all the many wet to mediocre ones that we in Britain optimistically plod through. And for the summer of 1976 they certainly pulled out all the stops.

Day after day the sun arced across a clear and cloudless sky; the wind, if it blew at all, was only in gentle zephyrs, while the sea remained like a sheet of deep blue glass. You lot want a good summer? Then try some of this. Neptune and his buddies really socked it to us that year. Johnny and I were working our boats as usual, and the pace was relentless. The weather was just so hot that people who wouldn't normally go boating ventured out just to enjoy the cooler air of the bay. Our little boats were running flat out from about ten in the morning, when people first strolled down to the quayside after their breakfast, until dusk when we called the last ones in from out of the gathering darkness. We had seven boats each, and at the slipway to seaward of us, Derrick Toms with Harry Pengelly worked a like number. While at the steps fifty yards to the north of us Claude Tamblin and brothers Stan and Darrel Hoskin operated their fleets. Freddie Lewis and Malcolm Solt worked from the steps one hundred yards north again. At Pearns boat yard above the bridge twenty five more were for hire. Collectively, about ninety 'doodle bugs' were plying from Looe, turning the harbour into what resembled a water-borne game of bumper cars The sound of summer was the massed pluttering of their Stewart Turner engines. Ninety boats for hire and people were queuing at the steps for them; we had never ever been so consistently busy, or ever sweated so much, running around in that heat. Seven days a week, week after week, we worked until one day I ended up with such a red raw sweat rash down between the cheeks of my behind. I was in agony and walking as if I had a nasty accident in the trouser area and I just had to have a day off to recuperate a little.

Charlie Butters was the boy working with me that year. I gave him his day's money and asked him to put the boats back on their moorings then, with a bandy legged gait, I hobbled back home. A day's rest did square me up a fair bit and the following morning as I was readying my boats, Johnny came over and passed me a bundle of money.

"What's this for," I enquired.

"Well," he said. "Yesterday we were so busy we were soon out of boats, so I sent the boy up after yours and we worked them as well."

I couldn't believe it, a man and a boy working fourteen boats, they must have been jumping around like meerkats on speed. But what a kind and thoughtful gesture. As the summer wore on, the heat baked the once green fields and gardens into shades of dull yellow and brown; tar melted in the roads and drinking water was rationed. Out on the cliffs the bracken and gorse first dried to tinder, then with a blaze it went afire, sending towers of black and grey smoke drifting up into the still air. It burned and smouldered for weeks the whole coast around, leaving behind acres of blackened land. And on a post high above the town, the fire siren wailed by day and night, calling to action the exhausted volunteer brigade time and again. Builders were starting work at five in the morning to avoid having to work through the punishing heat of the afternoons. Holiday makers and locals alike flocked for relief to the beaches, spending the day in and out of the sea trying to keep cool, the water feeling like a warm bath; careless sunbathers had the skin seared off of them, to peel away later in ragged pennants.

By night, the heat of the sun retained in the walls and roofs of many of the houses made sleep all but impossible, driving people to move outdoors to sleep on camp beds made up in backyards and on sheltered lawns. Brewers, lemonade factories and ice cream makers just couldn't keep pace with the demand. It must have been the weather they had all been collectively praying for, for generations.

And still the temperatures climbed ever upward, peaking finally at 110 Fahrenheit, at least that was the highest reading we experienced working on the quay. Then one day in late September this record breaking summer came to an end that was as dramatic as it had been hot.

A rain storm of tropical intensity was unleashed across the county, ending both the drought and the long hot summer. For one village, tucked tightly in its cliffside valley, this was going to be a night of horrors. A wall of flood water, backing up eight and ten feet deep in places, tore through Polperro. Many of the houses and cottages were devastated, flooded through from floor to ceiling, doors and windows ripped away and they, with the contents of the rooms, were to be found floating in the harbour the next morning, along with smashed up sheds, and battered cars, plus one body - that of an elderly gentleman swept to his death by the torrent that raged through his front room, carried from the hands of his daughter as she tried to guide him to safety.

It was a stark and shocking finish to a record breaking summer.

15

Scottish Invaders

I doubt there was ever a fishery that suited the Cornish fisherman as well as the hand line mackerel fishery. Any small fishing boat could be fitted out for it, and for a very modest outlay. Running expenses were low, and the returns (as in all branches of the fishing industry) matched the amount of hard work you were prepared to put into it. Those who worked the worst weather and the longest hours made the most money, and there were some very good wages to be earned. It was a selective fishery or, in the buzz word of today, very 'green'. If you stopped on a shoal of fish and tried your line only find that they were immature, you moved on until a shoal of mature ones was found. And there is no way that a fleet of hand liners, no matter how many there might be, could ever endanger a stock of fish. As with Cornwall's two other great fisheries, drift netting and long lining, their very method of operation guaranteed a healthy stock of fish for the next generation to earn a living with.

Simply because passive fishing methods, practised in small boats, ensured that both the fish and their habitats were not destroyed, men earned a living, not a fortune, and still left Mother Nature with the upper hand. But by the second half of the twentieth century all these methods were rapidly becoming obsolete. Modern fishing technology and development had now given man, for the very first time, the upper hand over nature, and for the marine environment that has proved to be very bad news indeed.

The story of the decline of the Cornish hand line fishery must begin in Norway, for it is here that they pioneered the research and development of the purse seine as an efficient way to catch herring. Its success was astounding, and it soon proved to be the ultimate way to catch any pelagic fish. The final development of the purse seiner was a highly specialised vessel that was as big as a coastal merchant ship that could encircle huge shoals of fish with a curtain of net in excess of a mile in circumference and as deep as any of the waters around the continental shelf.

With the aid of loans and grants from the Highlands and Islands development board, many of Scotland's leading fishermen invested in these purse seiners; one hell of an investment made by some very smart men. And indeed their forward thinking and hard work paid dividends, for an assault on the herring shoals could now be mounted like none that had ever been mounted before. Operated by skilled and dedicated fishermen, these vessels proved to be all too effective because by the early 1970s, the marine biologists published a report announcing that as far as they could calculate, the North Sea herring stocks had been so reduced as to be on the point of collapse and recommended an immediate ban on further catching to give the much depleted shoals a chance to regenerate. Accepting the scientists' findings, the government placed a three year ban on fishing for North Sea herring.

This ban, as necessary as it must have been, caused huge problems, because here were these massively expensive, highly specialised vessels (they could not turn to another method of fishing) tied up with nothing to do. It was not just the fishermen who would go bankrupt, the government (who had encouraged their construction), would also lose the many millions of pounds invested in them in the form of loans and grants. And so, to keep their boats running the Scotsmen came south, working out of Plymouth and Falmouth to try their luck on the mackerel shoals off the Cornish coast.

Against the Scots' fishing capability, the Cornish hand line fleet looked pathetic, a cottage industry. One Scots purser could catch more in a night than the whole Cornish fleet could land in a week. We had no chance, and neither were we given one. When news reached us that they were coming to Cornwall, there was uproar in the Cornish fishing fraternity; protest meetings were held and our MPs were lobbied. But there was precious little they could do. The Scots were British registered fishing vessels and as the law then stood, provided they stayed outside of the three mile limit, they were perfectly entitled to fish where and when they liked. We were assured that they wouldn't interfere with our operation as the market for their fish was very different from ours and they would be operating way out in the Channel. So, we were told, we had nothing to fear and really they were quite friendly and fluffy and would do us no harm whatsoever. Our collective answer to that was 'bollocks'. They had destroyed their own herring fishery up north, so given time why would they not destroy our mackerel fishery here in the south? And all the oily, platitude-peddling, lying bastards who were in authority at the time assured us that it would not go that way, and we in return told them exactly what we thought and so it proved.

The first of the Scots vessels to arrive probably couldn't believe their luck. From a few of miles off the coast to hard into the bays, the place was teaming with prime mackerel and night after night these huge seiners were loaded down to near sinking point. Of course, as word of their success spread, more and more of them came down to join in this bonanza. And it was not just purse seiners, every boat powerful enough to tow a mid-water trawl turned up, including a number of monster stern trawlers from Hull and Grimsby. These were the vessels that had done so much damage to the Arctic cod stocks that a war had been fought by Iceland to get them off of their fishing grounds. And here they all were, operating just a few miles off our coastline; vessels that, because of their size and power, had all but succeeded in wiping out the fishery that they had been built to prosecute.

The relentless slaughter of the mackerel shoals now gathered apace as day in, day out, fair weather or foul, thousands of tons of prime fish were brailed and pumped ashore from the holds of these mighty industrial fishers. Much of it was traded to a fleet of Russian factory ships (converted whalers) riding to their anchors in the Carrick Roads at Falmouth. While in Plymouth's Millbay Docks and at other wharfs around the Sound, refrigerated lorries lined up to load boxes of prime quality fish destined for the UK and continental markets, while the subprime stuff was convoyed away like so much manure, bound for the fish meal factories. In every area that these vessels operated in, the sea bed would be thickly carpeted with dead mackerel that they had somehow slipped or lost. Local trawlers hauled their nets to find them full to bursting point with stinking fish, hanging rotten from out of their skins, while the deaths of dolphins and pilot whales was also often in evidence.

The Cornish fishermen protested long and often, and to throw us a sop, half baked limits, checks and balances were put into place to be enforced by the local fishery patrol boats and a mine sweeper from the Royal Navy's fishery protection squadron. This proved to be about as effective as having a dead bulldog guarding a pile of money up a dark alley; they had rings run around them. Here was some very big business indeed, with money to match, and money talks. Fish merchants and hauliers had probably never had it so good. And while these big boys were leading the dance, our little boats in their harbours, making their irregular little catches, would have to take their chance. Because of the huge bulk of fish these industrial boats landed, they could afford to market their catches at bulk prices and still make a lot of money. But the hand liners needed a fair price for their fish, simply to make a decent average wage, because the winter gales could blow for days at a time when nothing could be earned. But business is business, and a merchant isn't going to pay a pound a stone for an uncertain supply of prime mackerel from the hand liners when a regular supply can be obtained from the pursers at fifty pence.

And so our prices tumbled, fifty pence for large fish down to five and ten pence for small, and of course our markets became less certain. Limits of one hundred and twenty stone per boat a day started to creep in, or we could land as much as we liked provided it was all large fish, and as we were now fishing on very mixed shoals, that was a nonsense. In the early days of the mackerel fishing the shoals were all in their year class, a shoal was either all small or medium or large and you would rarely catch mixed fish. But I think that probably because of the continual driving, harassing and slaughter of the fish, breaking up the big year class shoals, the survivors joined together for mutual self help. And no longer did they winter in the bays up and down the shore but instead they were often to be found well out to sea, flighty and always on the move. With their echo sounders going, the hand line fleet would put to sea in search of them, and it very often took many hours steaming about to locate a decent shoal, and then working like demons to try and load the boat down, because a hundred stone was no good now, the prices were much too low.

To add insult to injury we now acted as markers for the big boys, for when they slipped away from Plymouth or Falmouth, they only had to listen to their VHFs or switch on their radar to find the Cornish fleet sat over the fish they too were looking for. Our efforts must have saved them hours of searching because by late in the afternoon they would often be steaming around us sounding out the shoals we were on. Then they would just lay and wait for us to pack up for the day before wiping it out with a purse seine or smashing through it with a mid-water trawl. Sometimes they become impatient and would blow their fog horns, the skipper waving out of the wheelhouse window for us to clear off. Either way there would be nothing left for us to fish on the next day, meaning hours of searching to find yet another shoal for them to come out and decimate.

One morning the Cornish fleet was working a shoal of fish out off the Dodman when along came a Scots pair team on the hunt. They circled around the hand liners and then went out to seaward and shot their trawl, steering right at the shoal that we were working. This would have finished off our day's work because there would have been nothing left to fish on once they had been through it. Furious at their actions, I got on the VHF to one of the Falmouth boats, the skipper of which was a bit of a hot head, and suggested that for once we ought to fight back and not let these bastards have it all their own way. He agreed with me, and the upshot was that about twenty or so hand liners ceased fishing and steamed out to meet the pair trawlers. The Scots boats were big powerful craft, steel built and about seventy feet long. Our only chance to annoy them was to get ahead of them and slow right down to try and bring them to a halt. This in turn would make their gear sink to the bottom and they would have to haul it or risk fouling it on the rocks. But if the skippers held their nerve and carried on towing we would have to put the throttle on a bit quick to get out from under their bow before they sank us.

Tucked under the bow of a vessel like that is not a comfortable place to be but a couple of us went right in under the flare of each boat while the rest ranged alongside of them shouting and harassing like the angry men that they were. For a moment the Scotsmen looked astounded; they had never experienced this sort of treatment before. A man was up on each of their whalebacks shouting and waving back to the skipper in the wheelhouse as we slowed down and got ever closer to their great steel bows. It was a battle of nerves, but the Scotsmen's nerve went first and they slowed down and down until they stopped and had to haul their gear. The men in the surrounding boats had by now worked themselves up to a pitch of absolute fury and were threatening the Scots with everything from being flung overboard to murder if they ever caught them ashore. The Scots skippers could now be heard on channel sixteen shouting for the help of the fishery protection boat and reporting the incident ashore to the coastguards. Once their gear was hauled, they buggered off as hard as they could go and we, having won a small victory, went back to our day's fishing.

What we didn't expect was the publicity that that incident attracted. It was reported on the television news and in many of the national papers the next day. And by the dramatic way it was reported you would imagine the sea to be littered with dead bodies and wreckage. A sea battle had taken place between the Scots and the Cornish fishermen off the notorious Dodman Point etc, etc. In reality we had gained a few hours fishing that we wouldn't have had; the Scots had been rattled a bit, but doubtless they came back and slaughtered that shoal once we had left it. We the Cornish hand liners had vented our frustration and fury at what was happening to us, but in the end it made no difference.

Our markets were going, the fish were becoming much harder to find, and when we did find them it was mainly for the benefit of the opposition. By the middle of the 1980s the Cornish hand line industry was very fragmented; every harbour still had a fleet, but it shrank each successive season as men gave up and went ashore or looked elsewhere to earn a living, such as trawling or netting. The jobs that provided those vital winter wages were slipping away as boats' crews and fish packing gangs were no longer needed. But the Scotsmen were still out there earning big money, smashing up the shoals, carpeting the seabed with dead fish and sending thousands of tons of good fish to be made into fertiliser. That is progress, so it's okay then. No it wasn't, it was shameful crime that nobody in authority saw fit to stop.

16

The *Eileen*

In the spring of 1977 I sold my motor boats to buy the 44 foot lugger *Eileen*. Ernie Toms, her owner, had sadly passed on and his son Edward wanted rid of her to buy a smaller boat. She had been built in Looe in 1920 and packed two thirty HP Lister engines and, typical of the old drifters, both props came out of the port quarter. For the asking price of £2,000 she came complete with her summer sharking gear, mackerel gurdies for the winter fishing and plenty of assorted engine spares. The deal was done, and after giving the old vessel a good refit and paint up, crewman Don Lang and I spent a pleasant summer taking visitors out shark angling. We suffered a couple of minor breakdowns: a cylinder head cracked on one of the engines and another time the voltage regulator failed nearly setting the engine room afire, but it was all put to rights with very little loss of sea time. By mid September the holiday season was drawing to a close so Don and I made ready for the winter fishing, but with a boat of the *Eileen*'s size I needed at least two more crewmen. I put the word about and pretty soon had some results in the form of Mother's Lamb and Killer Combes.

Now Killer had a tidy reputation for thuggery, burgling, boozing and bullshit and for some of his more outrageous efforts he had enjoyed a few long holidays paid for by Her Majesty. Probably not long back from one of his holidays, he appeared on the quay one day.

"Morning Ned," he bellowed.

"Hello Mike, how are you doing?" I replied.

"Okay. I hear you are looking for crew. I'll come with you for the winter if you like."

To be honest I didn't like, not really, but what do you say to somebody like that. "If that's the case you had better come down aboard and give me and Don a hand to get the boat ready," I said with much more conviction than I really felt. And that was it, deal done. Mike Combes, 'Killer' to his friends and enemies (and he had plenty of both), shipped aboard for the winter.

I recruited the last hand at a party that weekend. Howard Bowden, the youngest son of a local well-to-do family fancied a go at the fishing, so I said I would give him a try. I think he was about eighteen at the time; he had a rather foppish air about him and spoke with a very posh Cornish accent. His mother, concerned for the well-being of her youngest son, once said to me, "I hope you will look after my Howard, because he is mother's lamb, you know." And that was it. He was 'Mother's Lamb' from then on.

I don't think I have ever been to sea with a more diverse set of characters than that winter on the *Eileen*. Don Lang, small and wiry of build, was in his late thirties, a pipe smoking mad inventor type, who could repair and maintain anything from a valve radio to a diesel engine. Mike Combes, in his early thirties, built like a brick chicken house and with a few pints down his neck he could be hell on wheels, but sober and at sea, he was a good worker. And last but not least, Howard Bowden, Mother's Lamb. On bad weather days at sea he would be back aft buried up in his oilskins, winding away on his gurdy, cold, wet and miserable. I would look aft and say, "All right, my Laaamb?" and he would glance from under his hood and go "Baaa" with all the pathos that sound could be made to carry.

With the *Eileen*'s cabin painted out clean and smart, and a coal stove installed to make it warm and cosy, we lived aboard for much of the winter, following the shoals of fish. We ranged the coast, landing our catches in Falmouth and Penzance. That was the only time I ever worked out of that port, in fact a small fleet of us operated from there, because Newlyn was full right up and just couldn't handle any more boats.

One morning, while in the usual process of hauling aboard endless lines full of fish, there came an anguished howl from the foredeck area. This was the mighty Killer announcing that he had a hook buried right in his hand. For a man who had made an art of being macho, he suddenly wasn't looking quite so tough. When a hook goes in past the barb you daren't think twice about it, it has to be ripped out there and then or you'll never do it and will spend the rest of the sorry day sat down in the cabin waiting to get ashore to see the doctor. Glancing up at Killer, who at that moment didn't quite know what he was going to do, I yelled at him, "For fuck's sake, we have just got into some good fishing and you have got a hook in your hand. Rip the bloody thing out and get on with it."

If looks could kill I should have been dead, but he ripped it out and carried on fishing with blood running out of his glove. The following day the same thing happened to me, but out it had to come, with no hesitation; I daren't after the way I had shouted at Mike. It wasn't the first or the last time I ever had to do that, but the pain of it fairly makes your eyes boggle. When the day's work was done and we were safely moored up for the night, we would sit around the cabin fire for our evening meal of pasties, pies or fish and chips, all washed down with a mug of tea, to be followed by an easy stroll ashore for a nightcap in the nearest pub. Don, with a pint of real ale would commandeer a comfy chair and smoke his pipe, talking cars or engines to somebody. I would be chatting to other fishermen about the day's events, while Killer would be at the bar, bigging it up as only he knew how. As for Mother's Lamb, he rarely if ever had a run ashore; a day at sea and he was totally knackered, stripped down to his leopard skin underpants, he would crawl into his sleeping bag soon after dinner, and that would be it until I roused him out the next morning.

One fog bound morning in Falmouth, all hope of going to sea abandoned, the *Eileen* was moored on the outside of a rank of boats at Custom House Quay. I was on deck squaring things up when I happened to catch sight of a stoutly built old boy in a dinghy working his way along the foreshore with a long handled hoe. It was low tide, and he was gazing down, picking up oysters in the shallow water. But what grabbed my attention was his little sausage dog companion, who was scampering from thwart to thwart, sticking his head over the side and barking fit to bust. Even at a distance the constant yapping was enough to drive you mad, but the old chap seemed not to notice it, and carried on hoeing up his oysters. As he drifted down past the *Eileen* I wished him a good morning and asked why his dog was so excited.

"He do look for Beaky," came the reply, as if I should know who Beaky was, and he carried on hoeing.

"Well, who is Beaky?" I asked.

"Beaky's a dolphin," he said, looking up from under the peak of his cap, "and lives around here. He do come alongside the boat to take my dog for a ride."

Oh yes, I thought. "And how does he do that then?"

"Well," he said. "He do lay alongside and I puts the dog on his back and Beaky takes him for a little trip out and around, and if the dog's not ready when Beaky arrives he's up over the side of the boat looking for him, barks like hell out on the dolphin as well, he does." With that he drifted off in to the fog.

Now this, I thought, was a yarn too far; a good one for the emmets, so I stowed it to the back of my mind. Maybe I would ask about that ashore later on. Enjoying a pint in the Chain Locker that evening, I got into conversation with one of the hovellers called Snowy, and mentioned this old boy and his dog and the dolphin. Snowy confirmed every word of the story and added many more to it. Beaky the dolphin was evidently very well known in Falmouth; he was an unbridled show off with a wicked sense of humour. That same old boy, Snowy told me, was one day trying to anchor his boat in the river to work an oyster dredge. Three times he flung the anchor away and as many times Beaky retrieved it and tossed it back aboard. At the fourth attempt the dolphin, instead of throwing it back, kept a grip of it and proceeded down the river at high speed towing the boat astern of him. The old chap was sat aft hanging on for grim death while his dog, right up on the stem, ears flapping in the breeze, barked his head off. They paraded down the river in this manner for a good half mile, looking like something out of Greek mythology, until Beaky, deciding that the joke was over, dropped the anchor and swam off.

This dolphin was known to have waited outside of Customs House quay when the mackerel boats were slipping away to sea in the dark of an early morning, going from boat to boat pushing them about. Some of the men were very nearly in need of clean trousers, momentarily convinced that something supernatural was happening to their boat. R N L I bigwigs and local dignitaries had gathered one day for the launching of a new high speed inshore lifeboat. The Mayor quacked at the crowd and champagne was poured. The gallant crew in full regalia then thundered off around the bay to showcase their new piece of kit. But it was Beaky who did the showing off; he stole their thunder entirely, for it was not 'Oh look at that boat!' but 'Oh look the dolphin!' Beaky was jumping from side to side high over the life boat.

He would play with the children swimming at Swan Pool beach and divers in the area lived in dread of him appearing, because he always insisted on rescuing them. The crew of the Irish purse seiner *Quo Vadis* stumbled into the bar of the Chain Locker one evening looking pale and frightened. Coming ashore in their RIB on a pitch dark night they found themselves being spun around in endless circles. Knowing nothing of Beaky, and being good Catholics, they were nearly ready to renounce all of their worldly goods and become monks if only the good Lord would show them some mercy. "That bloody fish frightened the soul case out of us," said the skipper. A ten minute run had taken nearly an hour.

Beaky became the talk of Falmouth, but one day he was gone. Where to, nobody knew. His japes had certainly been very amusing, providing of course you were an onlooker and not the one selected to take part in his idea of a fun time.

When the mackerel faded from the coast in late February we returned home to Looe, but it was a long time to try and live from then until June when the first holidaymakers put in an appearance. As a stop gap we had a go at long lining but there were just so many frustrations and uncertainties in that game and we gave it up. The biggest trouble was getting hold of fresh bait; there was a good supply of frozen mackerel available but it wasn't good enough. If we did get the bait, would the weather be fine enough, or would the tide be running too hard? It was a never-ending headache, something different had to be done.

I had worked the *Eileen* for a year and had made quite a decent living with her, but she couldn't be fitted for that vital third season, trawling, leaving a huge between-seasons gap where the money just drained away. And as well as that, after nearly 60 years of hard work, the old boat was getting rather tired. Both her engines were well worn, and she needed plenty of pumping when at sea in any weather. So, in the spring of 1978, I put her up for sale, having first spruced her right up, everything clean neat and freshly painted, with engines and all equipment aboard put into good working order. Of all people, a taxi driver from Plymouth bought her. He was full of what a wonderful fellow he was, and how much money he was going to make. Whether he did or not, I have no idea, but at the time he did have enough money to buy the *Eileen*.

I was now in the market for something of more recent construction that would fit the bill for our yearly three seasons. A little Scots ring-netter or a Devon crabber maybe, but definitely not another ancient Cornish lugger. After a month or more of scanning the boats for sale section in the *Fishing News*, and driving about looking at craft that over the phone sounded just fine, but upon inspection turned out to be little more than a tarted-up bundle of worn out old sticks (much like I had just got rid of), I was beginning to lose faith. My father, a shipwright by trade, kept mentioning the fact that the lugger *Ibis* was up for sale at Porthleven and suggested we go and have a look at her. I kept telling him that I had had enough of worn out old boats and wasn't interested.

This one, he said, was built by Percy Mitchell and anything built by him had got to be worth a look. So more to keep him happy and have a day out, I made arrangements to go and see her. Herbie Uren, the *Ibis*'s owner, met us in the car park at Porthleven, and the three of us strolled down to the harbour in the warm June sunshine. It was low tide, and his boat lay against the quay wall looking ill kempt and embarrassed. Climbing down a wall ladder we arrived on deck and it was not a very inspiring sight. Herbie was more of a boat killer than a maintainer, so after a few years in his tender care and a long lay-up, the *Ibis*, to put it mildly, was looking far from her best.

She was 42 feet long and had been built in 1930 by the best, and of the best, and for most of her life she had been well maintained. Her planking was of pitch pine, and each plank ran the full length of the hull and rang like a bell under Dad's little surveying hammer. Also, as with all Cornish boats of her era, she was of tight seam construction, so there were no butts to leak or caulking to fall out. The deck and bulwarks were serviceable, but the wheelhouse was rough and empty of gear; there was no sounder or radio, just a compass and the wheel. While down in the engine room sat a fine old eighty two HP Gardner diesel engine, worn but there was life in it yet. So beneath all the muck and neglect it seemed to me that a good boat was waiting to reappear. I was impressed and very surprised.

Herbie had gone back to his cottage while Dad and I did the surveying, so we wandered up to have a yarn with him. I was interested in his boat, but only if the price was right. It turned out that several fishermen had been to look at her but few had shown any real interest, and after many months of this, Herbie was by now desperate to be rid of her. Just the sort of vendor you need for driving home a hard bargain. I forget what his asking price had been, but I knew what I was prepared to pay, £2500, and on that the deal was struck.

I lodged at Porthleven for a couple of days while I made her fit to steam back to Looe. The poor old thing was full of junk and rubbish, the batteries were flat, the chain steering was ceased, etc, etc. But I managed to get everything working again and got her home without incident. I next laid her up for a few weeks to give her a good overhaul, fitting her out for the three seasons that we then worked. I obtained a fine old belt driven winch from Scarborough and brought it back to Looe via a relay of fish lorries. My father built and fitted a new wheelhouse and did any shipwright work that was needed, a few new stanchions in the bulwarks, capping rail etc. Pete the weld fabricated the trawling gantry and lead blocks, while Jack Statton the local engineer made up my mackerel gurdies. Next, a good paint up both inside and out really brought the old girl back to life, and as I had kept back all the fishing rods when I had sold the *Eileen* the *Ibis* was now ready to earn her keep once more.

I shipped up two crewmen, Nezzer and the Goat. Nezzer (his real name being Simon Keane) was sixteen years old and had just left school. The Goat (real name Neal Cumston) was in his early thirties, an ex-matlot and ex many other things as well, as crafty as a bag of weasels as his nickname implied, but as tough as hemp. Neither man had ever been fishing before so the winter of 1978/79 was a sort of shake down training period. Nezzer suffered with seasickness, while nothing whatsoever affected the Goat. After a week or so, both of them had got to grips with the mackerel fishing and were making a pretty good job of it as we chased the shoals from Bigbury Bay to the Lizard.

The *Ibis* proved to be a good boat, sound and seaworthy and, unlike most of the old luggers, she didn't leak in poor weather. I looked after her, and she in return never played me up. Over time I greatly altered the work I did with her, but I earned a living with the *Ibis* for the next 23 years. Come the early spring of 1979 we shipped up the trawl and went after the lemon-soles, working up off Plymouth and then south of the Eddystone and west on the clean trawling ground that lies to seaward of the reefs of rocks known as the Bretons and west again seaward of the Plashets, yet another collection of reefs. From there, we hauled out south a bit to clear the radar buoy and then west again passing the back of two wrecks, first the *Victoria* and then the *Silver Laurel*. By now the Dodman Point was handy and Falmouth Bay was in view; to go on any further required a more powerful boat and heavier gear as the ground became rough and uncertain with a very good chance of coming fast and tearing the trawl or worse still losing the lot. So in the early days of trawling, that was our ground.

17

Tragedy At Sea

A generation ago, the fishermen of Looe always maintained that God had got the port under his wing. This was because, despite of all the dangers in wresting a living from the sea in small boats in summer and winter, tragedies had mercifully been very few. But, as in every fishing port the world over, sooner or later someone's luck is going to run out, and when it does the effect is utterly devastating.

In January of 1979 a mackerel boat, the *Do It Again*, new to the port of Looe, had a small winch and gantry fitted to enable her to do a bit of trawling for those vital weeks at the end of the winter mackerel fishery and before the May month paint up. Being an open boat of only thirty feet long she was never going to be out deep working in any poor weather, but I suppose she might have scratched up a week's work up and down the shore in reasonable conditions.

One Saturday, towards the end of the month, the job was done and everything was aboard ready to go, so on the afternoon tide they slipped away for sea trials. This was to check that the winch was working okay and that the lead blocks were running fair, also to get some idea of what adjustments were needed to both trawl and trawl boards to get the gear working properly. John Haines was the skipper, a keen young chap just 19 years old, while his crew was Charlie Tregenna aged 17, the same lad who worked with us on the motor boats as a schoolboy. They shot the trawl away on the inside trawling ground, just a couple of miles off the shore and proceeded to tow down Channel with the tide. The weather was a bit fresh, SW 4-6, poor enough for her, but they were only going out for a couple hours and would have a fair run home before the sea.

That same afternoon, Jack Jollif, a retired fisherman from Polperro, was out strolling on the cliff path and happened to observe this little boat bashing her way slowly to the westward. Upon looking out again some minutes later he could no longer make her out. He was somewhat perplexed that she had apparently hauled her gear and gone from view in so short a time but continued his walk, although he was far from easy in his mind.

The Polperro boat *Westward*, skipper Bill Cowan and crew John Courtis, were out that day scallop fishing when they received a brief but desperate shout over the VHF radio: "Help, Do It Again." Bill snatched up the phone, broadcasting back: "Do It Again, this is the Westward, do you receive me?" There was only silence. He tried several more times but could not get a reply. He then shouted an open message over the air to try and find out if any other boats had heard that awful shout, but again there was complete silence. Not being familiar with the boat's name, Bill had no idea who she was or where the call might had come from, and as he could make no contact with any other vessels, there was nothing more he could do but carry on with his day's fishing.

Back in Looe, the parents of both boys knew that they were only out on trials and shouldn't be away for very long, but when darkness fell and they still hadn't returned, those dreadful pangs of doubt and worry started to gnaw at them. John's father spoke of his concern to his eldest son David who was a volunteer coastguard. From the coastguards' station, David tried time and again to contact his brother on the VHF but had no luck and, after making a few more checks as to their likely whereabouts and drawing a blank each time, he decided it was time to raise the alarm. Both Fowey and Plymouth lifeboats were launched to search for them, but the big problem was that nobody knew exactly where they had gone for their trials, east or west, on the inside or outside trawling grounds. Jack Joliff was the only witness to the *Do It Again*'s whereabouts but he was totally unaware of what was happening.

Knowing nothing of this unfolding drama, the Looe trawler *La Quete* nudged alongside the quay that evening. It had been a long and tiring day at sea and skipper Mike Soady and his crewman Leo Bowdler were glad to get their catch landed and go their separate ways home. Mike had just sat down to dinner when he received a call from the coastguards explaining the situation with the *Do It*

Again. He then phoned Leo to tell him what he had learnt. Both men then knew that, as weary as they were, they had to head back out to sea again and join in the search. There was no time to rouse others; if they didn't haste away immediately their boat would be aground on the tide.

At that time there would have still been the hope that maybe they had wrapped the trawl in the propeller and needed a tow in, or that they had come hard and fast and were awaiting the turn of the tide to get the trawl free, but why hadn't they answered the radio calls? Or called others to let them know what they were doing? Things were not adding up. Early the next morning the quay was abuzz with the dreadful news, and as we made our boats ready for sea, everyone knew that a very grim day indeed lay ahead of us all. The two lifeboats and the *La Quete* had been searching through night and had found nothing. It was all so sad. By daybreak word had spread as boats from Polperro, Fowey and Mevagissey joined us, line abreast, doing a sweep search up and down the coast, hour after hour, looking for any sign at all of the missing *Do It Again* and the boys that were on her. We knew by then that she had gone, but it was the how and the why and the where that needed answering, and most urgent of all, to try and locate the bodies of her poor drowned crew. For the sake of their grieving families it was paramount that they be found but secretly, for the sake of your own nightmares you wished that honour on others and not yourself.

And then a shout went up on the VHF. It was Bill Wadling, skipper of the *Our Daddy* announcing that he had located a body floating close to his starboard bow and was going to try and retrieve it. One of the lifeboats told him to hold fast, they would come over and lift the body as they had the gear to do so. Praises be! One found, one to go. The fleet searched on, up and down, in and out with no further result, neither could we locate the wreck on our echo sounders, for the thought was that maybe the other man, Charlie (for it was John, the skipper's body that had been found), might be trapped in the cabin.

By sundown we had abandoned the search and returned to harbour, the end of a sad, sad day. Mike Soady on the *La Quete* decided to see the week out searching for Charlie and the wreck while the rest of the fleet returned to the fishing. Inadvertently, any boats working the inside trawling ground were also helping with the search as well, as there are few things better than a trawl to bring up anything laying on the sea bed. And so it was that a few days later, Ivan Chaston and Eric Brown on the *Tethera* were towing their trawl when, on a previously clear piece of ground, they came fast. As they winched back to retrieve the gear. Mike Soady came over in the *La Quete* and marked the obstruction on his sounder. There it was as plain as a pike staff; it had to be the wreck of the *Do It Again*. Ivan danned off his gear while Mike contacted the Navy in Plymouth.

The next day a team of divers from the bomb disposal squad went down to take a look, and when they surfaced they confirmed that the wreck had been found. First they cleared Ivan's trawl away and then attached some surface marker buoys. The divers then cradled the hull with two lifting strops so that the wreck could now be raised.

The following day, as the weather still held fine, Polperro skipper Kevin Curtis manoeuvred his powerful ex-French trawler the *Veronique* over the wreck site and sent down two heavy nylon warps. The divers waiting below on the wreck then shackled them to the lifting strops, checked and checked again that all was ready, then sent a signal to the surface for the lift to begin. Aboard the *Veronique* the winch was engaged, first to take up the slack and then, after a final check with the divers below that all was well, the lift commenced. The engine slowed a few revolutions, working hard to power the winch, its drive belt joining links, clack-clacking as they hit the jockey wheel. The warps hissed water, singing like harp strings as they passed through the gantry hanging blocks, the old trawler now under considerable strain, cluckied down a couple of planks lower in the water as the wreck rose up to meet her. Kevin lifted the *Do It Again* as tight up under his boat as he could and then at high tide the *La Quete* towed him into Talland Bay. There, in shallow water, the wreck was lowered to the bottom to allow the divers to attach lifting bags and draw her into where she would be exposed at low tide. When this had been achieved, the surveyors inspected her to try and come to a verdict as to why she had sunk. First of all there was no body in the cabin, and secondly, after endless debate and deliberation, no really hard and fast evidence was ever found or conclusion drawn as to what had caused the fateful sinking. It remained an open verdict.

One theory amongst the fishermen at the time was that her gantry looked proportionally high for a small boat and that maybe she had capsized, but tests carried out proved that it was not so. And again, if John had enough time to broadcast a brief distress call then strip off his clothes to swim, why were the life jackets and life raft left untouched. But exactly how do you react when suddenly traumatised and facing the prospect death? Not always logically I suspect. There are many questions that were, and now always will remain unanswered.

The tragic loss of those two young Looe fishermen plunged the whole community into mourning, and when skipper John Haines was laid to rest it was standing room only in the church, while the sorrow and utter heartbreaking grief of that occasion I just cannot begin to convey in words. When the body of young John was brought in from the sea, at least the Haines family could hold a funeral, enabling them to draw something of a line under the tragedy, although it could do nothing to ease the grief of their loss. But for the Tregenna family there was no such solace; their son Christopher (Charlie had been his nickname) was still missing at sea. For months they lived in fear and expectation of a phone call informing them that somewhere, somehow, his remains had been discovered.

It was six months before the sea gave up its dead. Remains that were later identified as that of Christopher were found washed up on a beach in Whitsand Bay.

18

Mounts Bay

The winter of 1981/82 was a very tough time in many ways. The mackerel season had failed in the Looe and Falmouth areas and the only 'scry' we knew of was in Mounts Bay. So, after weeks of scratching about earning very little, most of the Looe fleet steamed westward around the Lizard to work out of Newlyn, a rugged old port to work from in the winter time. The Atlantic ground swell can run like an endless procession of undulating hills with an angry top wash overlaying it, created by whatever wind was venting its anger at the time. Two boats, one each in a trough either side of a sea, would be out of sight of one another, maybe even the mast heads hidden from view. But if the choice was to stay at home and go into debt, or work out of Newlyn there's no choice. Newlyn it was.

The harbour in those days was jam-packed with boats. There was a fleet of beamers, stern draggers, side-winders, long liners and netters, and in addition it was also playing host to a couple of hundred mackerel boats from all around Cornwall. I have heard the old men talk of the herring fishing days when harbours were so busy you could walk across them from boat to boat. Well, that was Newlyn that winter. Boats were moored in tiers twelve or sixteen deep off the quay and scrambling across from boat to boat to get ropes ashore was a nightmare after a hard day at sea. And on the occasions that a gale raged in from the south-east, ropes and fenders had to be continually attended to as these huge tiers of boats slewed about in the wind, while waves and spray bursting over the harbour wall put the smaller open boats in danger of being sunk.

The crews of most of the visiting craft lived within reasonable commuting distance of Newlyn and would rattle back and forth daily in a shaky assortment of cars and vans. Unfortunately, Looe was just too far away to do that, so we all had to stay in Newlyn for the week, going home for the weekend late on Friday afternoon and returning again early on Sunday morning. In some of the vehicles we had in those days, journeying from Looe to Newlyn could be an event, not quite the sort of trip you packed a blanket, a flask of tea and sandwiches, but not far off.

The men on the larger deck boats such as my *Ibis*, the *Maret*, *Prosperity* and the *Gratitude* lived aboard, as we all had decent cabins with comfortable bunks and a coal fire to keep things warm and dry. Certainly it was rough and ready living, and a world away from the word luxury, but we were all used to that way of life and didn't consider it to be a hardship one bit. While the crews of the smaller Looe boats, such as the *Ganesha*, *Claire*, *Seabird*, *Paula* etc. only had tiny fore peak cuddies that were usually shared with the engine. They were okay to sit in and have your grub, or as somewhere to get in out of the weather for a bit and warm up, but they were such that I rather suspect a skipper would have been up on a charge of cruelty if he tried to keep a rat in there for the winter, let alone his crew. To solve the problem, two or three crews would band together to rent a flat or a cottage; an extra expense but at least they had somewhere decent to live.

When working out of a harbour as busy as Newlyn, landing your catch at the end of the day could take ages. Boat after boat would be ranked off the quay, loaded down with mackerel, the crews all busy grading, washing and boxing up. Perilously loaded fish lorries would be trundling back and forth to the packing sheds, all to a background noise of boats' engines, V.H.F radios and the laughter and back chat of the men. Eventually your turn would come to get your fish ashore, loaded on to the lorry and all tallied up. 'Thank God for that' was the usual sort of utterance as you manoeuvred away from the hustle and chaos of the landing berths, to go and moor up for the night.

Once the ropes and fenders were out and the old boat was safe, it was off with smock and overalls, a swill off in the deck bucket and then ashore for a meal and a pint. Food-wise there were two choices: fish and chips or a Chinese take-away, so we used to go day about, bearing our greasy paper-wrapped meal into the fishermen's mission where we could buy a mug of tea to wash it down with. Once dinner was over there were a couple of choices as to how the rest of the evening could be spent. A stroll about the quayside to let your dinner go down and then back aboard the boat for an early night was one option, not a very attractive prospect when you are a young man, or a pint or two at the Star Inn. Now that sounded much more like it. And many a good night we spent in there, yarning of the day's events with other fishermen, singing the old songs, dancing to the juke box or playing darts and cards, while the drinking often carried on long after closing time. Then, glowing from both the drink and the events of the evening, we would stagger out into the cold night air and down to the harbour side where the first problem for a beer-befuddled brain was to try and remember which particular rank of boats yours was tied up in. When that was sorted, the task of getting aboard began, up down, over and across all different shapes and sizes of craft, trying to avoid dodgy deck boards, unshipped hatches, pound boards, gurdies and boxes. Half cut and in the dark, this could be quite a challenge. The ultimate piss off was to reach the outside boat not having found your own, for the simple reason you were in the wrong tier. Now that really could cause a sense of humour failure.

After twelve or fourteen hours hard labour and a gut full of beer, sleep came just minutes after you scrambled into the bunk. It was the alarm clock jangling away at five o'clock in the morning that was the problem: oh the thick head and the aching limbs. The crew emerge from their bunks, bleary-eyed, scratching and farting, to pull on damp and dirty overalls, smocks and hats, followed by their sea boots, then to clamber up on deck to take a look at the day. It was usually dark, wet and cold with a fresh wind blowing from somewhere in the westerly cant. Surrounded by the noise of engines grinding and roaring into life, fogging up the harbour with billows of thick oily exhaust, navigation lights glowing, deck lights twinkling, there is banter and chatter as ropes are cast off. Boats are steering for the pier head gaps and away out to sea. It's time to go; the gurdies are passed up from the fish room and clamped onto the rail, then oilskins are chucked up from the engine room. These were full length things made of canvas backed PVC, perpetually cold wet and slimy, and to don them you always had to fight your way in, hands punching into the sleeves, head nodding and shaking to get up into and through the neck; they stank inside of diesel and stale fish and felt like armour to wear. And there we would be, ready for action. With mooring ropes and fenders stowed, we would join the procession of craft making for the harbour entrance.

In the dark of the wheel house I keep a sharp lookout as we steer up across the bay, the boat lifting to the ground swell and throwing back cat's paws of spray from the wind-blown top wash. Nezzer is perched on the seat behind me, while down in the cabin, the Goat is hunched over the fire, smoking a fag and reading a girlie mag as he waits for the kettle to boil. The forecast is far from good, in fact it's fucking awful, but if we can work away head to wind in some steady fishing the weather won't be too much of a problem. Daylight begins to creep into the sky and that makes things feel much better; on the VHF a few skippers are talking of decent marks on the sounder up off Porthlevan, so it's hoist the mizzen and bend on a new set of feathers. The day's labour will soon begin.

The white trace paper of the echo sounder slowly winds across the illuminated screen, the stylus on its rubber belt faithfully recording the depth of water and shoals of fish as it blurs around with a scratch, scratch, scratch sound. A few peppery marks, known as fly shit, show up, then some nice big swipes, top to bottom of the paper, and a bit further on the screen is blacked out with solid fish. The first boats away are already riding head to wind above this lot, as are the gannets; both men and birds are awaiting the daylight to penetrate down into the water. As light chases dark over the western horizon the birds take to the air, we drop our lines, still too early yet; we foul hook one or two but can feel mackerel in their hundreds hitting on the lines. We breakfast on tea and pork pies, glancing to weather; a teasy wind kicks up sea bobs while the sky, heavy with great billowing clouds, backs the forecasters' predictions, south west six to gale eight. A boat nearby pulls a line full of big mackerel aboard. Daylight is at last in the water and the gannets are going berserk.

Two hundred boats, from fifty to twenty feet long, lie head to wind, bows rising and falling on the sea, mizzens hauled up as tight as drum skins ripple in the freshening breeze. Their crews toil ceaselessly to get as many fish aboard as they can before the worsening weather conditions drive them back to port. By early afternoon the wind-blown top wash starts to heap up the ground sea. It's all looking very ugly. If the forecasters are right we shall be confined to harbour for several days while the storm lashes its way up Channel, so as much as possible has to be squeezed out of this day.

Good steady fishing on decent quality fish tempted us all to work for much too long into a rising gale, and by the time we did get under way daylight was often rapidly fading and conditions were wild to say the least. Keeping a watch three waves ahead gave you time to pick out the seas that were going to give you trouble: the high, wall-fronted combers that were just about to break or that were already breaking, they were the ones. So it's ease down the engine and wind down the wheel to take them fine on the luff of the bow. Up she rises, bow pointing skyward, spray lashing the wheelhouse like a power hose, swooping down into the trough on the other side, it's just green water all around and the sky above, and up again on the next one and now it's big rollers all about you and okay to get back on course once more. In such conditions it is patience, tenacity and good seamanship that get you back to harbour safe and sound.

But however good the boat handling and however sharp the lookout, every now and then a sea so steep, big and horrible that you know you can do nothing with it, will roll your way.

"Hang on tight boys!" is a typical shout as something that could well be your doom breaks over the boat. Stopped dead in its tracks and buried under tons of boiling angry sea, the boat is now fighting for her life. Wallowing and rolling, she climbs up out of it awash to the gunnels, shaking like a gundog emerging from a river, the scuppers streaming like waterfalls. Fight it, girl, fight it, you say to encourage the boat, because if another sea like that drops on us before she frees herself we will all have had it. But, thank God, that doesn't happen. Everything is working and everything is still intact, so you plough on again.

Such a sea caught us that night. Enough water went down the cabin chimney to wash the fire clean out of the stove, leaving the sole a crunching, gritty mass of wet coal and ash. In fact the whole cabin was awash, even the clothes and bedding in the bunks were wet and soggy. One or two of the small open boats were very fortunate to get back to port at all that night. The Looe boat *Sandy D*, just twenty four feet long, got caught broadside in the tube of a large breaking sea, just like a surfer. Mike Darlington, the skipper, thought for a moment that they had had it, but they shot out the other end of the tube, intact and unscathed - a minor miracle. Broadside to weather, two hundred heavily laden boats fought their way home in the dark across a storm-lashed Mounts Bay, and for some it was a very close call. But battered and weary, they all made it back to land their catches.

Working from Newlyn that winter, there were a few fine days fishing making it a pleasure to be out on the water, but as I remember it the living was mainly very hard won.

Just before Christmas there was the terrible tragedy of the lifeboat *Solomon Brown*, lost with all hands. Wreckage from her was brought ashore and laid out on the quayside, while the crippled coaster the *Union Star*, whose crew they had gone to rescue, was smashed against the cliff, hull up, and they too had perished. All of Newlyn and Mousehole went into mourning and at the same time, they had to try and deal with the huge media circus that it attracted; everyone wanted a piece of that disaster. Like a snapshot in my memory, I shall always recall the two old men I observed hunched over a table in the Newlyn fishermen's mission, talking closely and quietly together, their weather beaten faces, drawn and gaunt, as if on the point of tears. The ritual of rolling, lighting and smoking cigarettes provided a vital prop for both time and dignity. Several years previously one of them had lost a son at sea from a trawler, and he was now trying to comfort his friend who had just lost a son on the *Solomon Brown*.

Fine, brave old men, battling a mountain of heartbreak as so many other people were doing in Newlyn and Mousehole.

19

Loss Of The *Claire*

We fished from Newlyn until the mackerel shoals thinned out late in January of the new year, then all the visiting boats headed back to their home ports. It was a lovely day when the *Ibis* at last departed and as we were turning in the harbour, a shout from the quay caught our attention. It was Ernie George who was crew on one of the other Looe boats, the *Seabird*. For some reason he had not gone home on her, and now jumped aboard us for a lift up to Looe. Catching the first of a young spring flood, we fairly romped up the coast and on rounding the Lizard we had none of the usual jump and bash that the headland is so famous for. Instead we glided around in comfort, mugs of tea in hand, enjoying the afternoon sunshine. Ernie's family had originated from the Lizard area and he spun us many a tale of the cliffs, farms and houses there as we sped around.

The run up to Looe that day took six and a half hours, a very smart run for those times. It was good to be back in our home port again. Back with the family for a home-cooked meal and an evening by the fireside instead of fish and chips and the Star Inn, to sleep in your own warm comfortable bed rather than in your bunk, lying fully clothed under a damp blanket. Luxury indeed after weeks of fishing away.

But a living still had to be earned, and it was now our trawling season. All the mackerel fishing equipment, mizzen, gurdies etc were put back into the store and we greased up the winch to wind on the warps and combination, chain the doors up to the gantry and stowed a couple of trawls aboard. We would now be hunting whiting, plaice, monk and lemon-sole instead of the mackerel; a different trade, a different season.

We soon got into the swing of the trawling, and there were plenty of fish to be caught on the home grounds just a half an hour's steaming from port. A four hour tow would result in a mixed bag of fish: whiting, squid, monk, plaice and hake plus a few odds and sods such as conger, spur dogs and ray. Sometimes we would only just get the catch gutted, washed and graded in time for the next haul and then start all over again. Big catches gave a good feeling, but when you are up to your arse in fish so are all the other boats, and it is then that the prices paid by the buyers on the market take a dive.

When trawling, the best wages were always earned with a modest catch of quality fish landed two or three times a week, between the winter gales. The buyers always paid the best money when they were in a state of hair-tearing desperation and fully prepared to cut each other's throats to get enough fish to fulfil their customers' orders. Happy complacent fish merchants are no good to fisherman whatsoever.

A new method of fishing using monofilament netting was finding favour. We had seen boats at Newlyn using it to catch spur dogs, but nearly any species of fish could be caught with the right size mesh. Mike Faulkner of the *Claire*, among others, thought it held some good prospects and had rigged up several fleets of it to catch ling, pollack and cod that were to be found on and around the rocks and rough ground where the trawlers couldn't work. For the maiden shoot, Mike and his crewman Roger Davis had picked a nice fine day. We on the trawlers were at sea, still fishing the inside ground. While the *Claire* was steaming out to the reefs just to seaward of where we were working, I heard the skipper chatting on the VHF saying that he wouldn't be out for long as they were only going to shoot a few fleets away over the rocks to try the gear, and then they would be going back to harbour. And that was it, he was never heard again.

The trawler *Tethera* was the nearest boat to the *Claire* and could see her going from reef to reef shooting away her gear, and then she stopped and just drifted broadside to the light easterly breeze. For a short while there was nothing particularly odd about that. They might have had a bit of trouble with an engine or a pump and had let the boat blow away while they sorted it out. Aboard of the *Tethera*, Ivan Chaston and his crewman Eric Brown kept an eye on the *Claire*, but after an hour they began to suspect all was not well and tried to raise her on the VHF. Again and again they tried. Something was not adding up, so Ivan and Eric hauled their trawl and motored out towards the *Claire* to find out what the trouble might be, trying all the while to raise them on the VHF and still getting no reply. As they approached the boat they could see that her engines were running, but nobody was visible on deck. At first it was assumed that the crew must be in the fore peak sorting something out, but what they couldn't imagine. Ivan put the *Tethera* close alongside and hailed her two or three times to no avail. By now things were not looking good at all. Eric rigged the fenders and Ivan put his boat hard alongside the *Claire* for Eric to jump aboard and investigate. It took but a moment for Eric to realise that the crew was missing. The boat was fine, engine ticking over, echo sounder running - in fact, nothing out of place and no sign of any trouble.

Ivan raised the alarm immediately, calling up Leo Bowdler, the skipper of another Looe trawler, the *Maret*, that Mike's brother Johnny crewed on. I remember that call as if it was yesterday: "Maret, Maret, Tethera. Get up here a bit quick. Tell Johnny that we have just come up to have a look at the Claire and no one's aboard her".

Every boat in the fleet heard that message, and every skipper there and then gave orders to haul the gear. Within ten minutes or so everyone was racing up to the *Tethera*'s position to begin a search. As there was nothing wrong with the *Claire*, Eric had taken her back to port. The first thought was that somehow Mike and Roger had been pulled overboard in an accident while shooting their nets, so skipper John Andrews on another netter, the *Ma Cheri*, proceeded to haul the *Claire*'s gear, but it was all in good order and nothing was fouled in it. Meanwhile a big search had got underway, every fishing boat from all the surrounding ports within a reasonable steaming distance joined in, plus the Plymouth and Fowey lifeboats and a Royal Navy frigate.

As with the loss of the *Do It Again*, everyone formed up line abreast one Decca tenth apart and proceeded to comb the area, while Mike Soady in his trawler *La Quete* once again acted as the fleet coordinator. When darkness closed about us we still carried on the search, illuminating our way with searchlights and flares, until on a falling tide we had to abandon our quest and return to harbour to land our fish and make ready to resume the search again at first light the next day.

On the following day, word had spread of the loss of the crew of the *Claire* and a huge fleet of craft assembled to join in the hunt for the bodies of Mike Faulkner and Roger Davies. Lifeboats, Royal Navy frigates and fishing boats from Plymouth, Cawsand, Polperro, Fowey and Mevagissey all joined the Looe fleet in its sad and tragic mission. All through the daylight hours we boxed about, in, out, up Channel, down Channel and all to no avail. So many boats had so thoroughly covered such a huge area that we knew that if there was anything to be found someone would have done so. There was now no point in looking further; the bodies of Mike and Roger must have sunk to the bottom. All we could do now was go back to our fishing and maybe eventually, for the sake of the families, someone would bring their remains home.

For the rest of that winter, every time the trawl was hauled we lived in dread of finding a body in the cod end. As with the *Do It Again*, everyone wanted the men to be found but hoped the task would fall to others. And so it was that about six weeks later, John Kitto and his crewman Jim Gowan on the *Bev-An-Dan* hauled their trawl to find an oilskin-clad corpse among the fish in the cod end. As reverently and gently as possible, the trawl was lowered down onto the deck where John took a sharp knife to split the cod end open. The body was carefully eased out from among the fish and laid in the waterways. John was sure it was Mike Faulkner, and it later proved to be. The coastguards were informed of the sad find before the *Bev-An-Dan* headed back for Looe, where they were met by the police and the local undertaker.

The body was later positively identified by a wedding ring as Mike. He left behind his wife Bette and two young children, Tracy and Kevin; and to add to the heartbreak Roger Davies, the missing crewman, was Bette's brother. That poor family had to shoulder a burden of grief that must have been almost too heavy to bear. High up on the Downs overlooking West Looe is a graveyard, and it was there that we said farewell to skipper Mike Faulkner of the *Claire*.As far as I can recall there was no church service, instead hundreds of mourners lined the cemetery for the burial service and to pay their last respects.

Mike and I had crewed together on the old lugger *Iris*, pilchard drifting back in the 1960s, and had shared many a pint and a yarn at the Star Inn at Newlyn only weeks before when the Looe fleet fished the winter mackerel shoals in Mounts Bay. After the funeral, the *Claire* and all her equipment was sold at an auction held under the fish market and to raise extra money, many of the skippers donated what gear they could spare, nets and trawls etc. Some of it was not much good at all, but every item made very good money.

Of poor Roger Davies, no trace was ever found. He was a single man, a shipwright by trade, with no dependant, but he was part of a large family and is sorely missed to this day. The cause of their loss may never ever be known, but the conclusion that most have drawn is that one man somehow fell overboard and, in trying to rescue him, the other was dragged in as well. There would be no way to get back aboard after that, a scenario to awful to dwell on. A couple of years later the *Claire* also met her end, wrecked on the Rannies, a treacherous reef the eastern side of Looe Island. Fortunately there was no loss of life on that occasion.

20

Shark Fishing

In the days that I write of, there was plenty of fish to catch most of the time and a fisherman's life was free and independent. We chased the mackerel shoals the length of the coast, working from Plymouth to Newlyn, and when they disappeared from the coast in late February we wound on the trawling gear to have a go at the lemon-soles for a few weeks before the spring paint up. After a couple of summer seasons, Nezzer sat his skipper's ticket, so that he and the Goat could take the boat out shark fishing while I stayed on the quay getting customers to keep the *Ibis* running, fully booked, seven days a week.

I wasn't the only one on the quay booking trips. Dave Haines, Louis Portman and Ian Giddings booked their boats for mackerel fishing and evening conger trips. Each skipper had a sign-written board about four feet by eighteen inches that displayed the boat's name and details of the trips they were plying, plus a little note book for people to sign for the trip that they fancied. There was also a blackboard that was used to chalk up the forecast and advertise river trips when the weather was too poor to go to sea. Also, for our amusement, completely fictitious events would be neatly written up in eye-catching colours. Visitors were invited to attend the annual display of the Downderry over-eighties nude formation hedgehog-squatting team. A musical evening put on by the Respryn Bridge singing donkeys, performing negro spirituals and songs from the shows. Or maybe a cruise up the river to the wildlife park, there to view mock turtles, clockwork lobsters, unicorns and Cornwall's only colony of ooo-me-goolie birds. There was conger-wrestling, a wrecked pasty ship and underwater fag-rolling, to list just a few of the spoof trips we used to chalk up, and watching people discovering this was always amusing. Reading down the line of boards, they would be offered mackerel fishing, a coastal cruise to Polperro, shark angling, and what's this? Clockwork lobsters? Singing donkeys? Then the penny would drop and it was big laughs and the camera would come out. Staff from the shops would stroll by in their lunch hour for a giggle, and if a trip was up for more than about two days there would be demands for a new one. We were forever racking our brains, but we did come up with some corkers between us, each one dafter than the last.

We even had some serious enquiries, such as, "We hope there was no cruelty involved in teaching those donkeys to sing?" And, "Is it half price for kids at the conger-wrestling?" A sense of humour was vital, especially if somebody pulled what we called a 'stumper' on you. A skipper would bring his boat to the steps to pick up his people and as he was pulling away again someone would shout out to him, "Don't forget your probation officer wants to see you later on," or "Try and keep clear of the killer whales, this time." With good timing and using the right tone of voice, the skipper would be left trying to explain to his somewhat unsettled passengers that it was only a jape. Many is the day there was much more fun going on than work.

That was our year, our three seasons; we earned a good living and enjoyed what we did, but by the mid 1980s things were on the change, and certainly not for the better. Because of the activities of the big Scots industrial fishers, it was becoming ever more difficult to make a regular living from the mackerel seasons so more time had to be spent trawling, a trade that I had only ever enjoyed as a stop gap. The hours spent towing along watching the Decca clocks tick around drove me to distraction and instead of flying by, the day never seemed to end. But like it or loath it, of all the fishing methods, a steady living could always be earned with the trawl. And by now many of the Looe skippers were getting rid of their mackerel boats and buying vessels more suitable for trawling. Some invested in brand new boats, heavily built wooden craft 35 to 40 feet long, many of them launched from Alan Toms' yard at Polruan, or Gerald Pearn's yard at Morval. Others preferred secondhand craft, and a popular choice were the little cruiser-stern Scots built boats like Bonzo's *Prosperity*.

Trawling was a very new trade to most of the Looe fishermen, so there was an awful lot to learn. Charlie Jaycock, Ivan Chaston and Bill Hocking were the only three skippers who knew much about

106

it and their advice was always being sought on how to set the gear up and what type of trawl and trawl doors were best to use. Their experience and advice at this juncture was invaluable. Another man who put a lot of time and effort in to helping out those who were novices at the trade was retired fisherman Jack Soady, known to all as Uncle Jack. On bad weather days Jack would be going from boat to boat all day long, teaching baffled fishermen how to rebuild a badly damaged trawl, knife and needle always at the ready. And when the fleet was at sea he would spend his days in the store making and designing new trawls to order, or repairing nets that had been badly ripped up. For many years he was very much a father figure to the growing Looe trawler fleet, and he carried on working well into his eighties. A kind and jovial man who asked not a penny for all the help he gave, when he made a trawl he charged only pocket money prices.

At this time, all trawl fish landed at Looe was transported by lorry to be auctioned on Plymouth fish market. Looe had once had its own market but that had closed when the long-line fleet declined in the 1950s. But now, once again, tons of prime fish were being landed weekly on Looe quay by a fleet of boats that was expanding rapidly and becoming ever more efficient. These boats were now losing thousands of pounds a year because landing dues had to be paid at both Looe and Plymouth, plus overland fish was always sold last on the market and made the lowest price. And being last to be sold at Plymouth, especially in the summer time, could be disastrous for the quality of the fish at the old Victorian market, open to both sun and wind.

With this in mind, a deputation of the more forward thinking skippers petitioned the Looe harbour commissioners, led by its chairman, skipper Mike Soady, to give serious consideration to the re-opening of Looe auction market. This was a bold move. To reopen the auction market didn't just entail scrubbing out the old one and luring a few fish buyers back to Looe. Far from it, this was going to be a huge operation. A brand new market would have to be built with all modern facilities, chill rooms, offices, packing stores etc. The commission was at first a little wary of such a huge commitment but eventually, under the strong leadership of their chairman, they got behind the scheme. Finance, in the form of loans and grants, was sourced from many different organisations, plans were drawn up and scrutinised, hundreds of letters were written and thousands of phone calls were made. Committees and sub-committees held endless meetings, some quiet affairs where things were nodded through, while others became quite heated. But regardless of the differences of opinion, they knew that they dare not fail, as the vast majority of the Looe fishermen were now behind the idea. Eventually, plans were agreed and passed, the finances were in position and stage one, building the new market, could go ahead. But before anything new could go up, a lot of old stuff had to come down; in fact, a huge area of the quay had to be cleared. The old fish market and net lofts, mackerel packing sheds and assorted old tin huts were all levelled by the demolition gang with their iron dinosaurs and monster lorries. And suddenly a huge area of the quay was level and empty, while quite a number of houses and cottages found they now had magnificent uninterrupted harbour views. I hope they enjoyed it.

The construction gang came on site, driving huge piles down through the quays, followed by lorry loads of concrete that cast the foundations. Steel erectors with their crane bolted together a massive skeleton which, when finished, was fleshed out by teams of masons, chippies, roofers, plumbers, electricians and painters. Each in their turn helped to create and complete our brand new fish market.

This brief description glosses over what in reality was months of hard work, and it didn't always go smoothly. There were the usual delays, mistakes, misunderstandings and general balls ups that on occasions led to some truly magnificent displays of frustration. But all came together in time for the grand opening in October 1987. This ceremony was performed by the chairman of the harbour commissioners, Mike Soady, who (looking rather uncomfortable trussed up in suit and tie) made a short speech welcoming guests and dignitaries before unveiling a plaque to commemorate the occasion.

The second stage was the building of the fish packing units and offices, an imposing construction that at the time proved to be rather controversial. Completed by 1990, the guest of honour at the opening ceremony was our local MP, Sir Robert Hicks. Faith in the Looe fleet was not misplaced; the market took off from the word go and at its peak a few years later, 27 trawlers were working from the port, plus a handful of netters and crabbers. Trucks and lorries brought fish to the market overland from Polperro, Mevagissey, Newquay etc. It soon built a reputation for top quality day caught fish, supplying customers the length of the country, plus a booming export trade to Europe. Much of the market's success was down to the management skills and business acumen of the Blue Sail Fish company run by Steve Farrah and Hugh Symonds. A market can be built, but someone has got to have the know-how to run it. They were definitely the right men in the right place at the right time.

East Looe Quay was now a hive of activity for virtually 24 hours a day. In the small hours of the morning, long before daylight greys the eastern sky, the boats will be slipping away to sea, while on the market, staff will be laying out the previous day's catch ready for auction. Lorries wanting to load or unload arrive and depart all through the day, keeping a gang of market workers toiling with pallet truck and fork lift. In the packing sheds, fish merchants jabber on their mobile phones, taking orders for their staff to weigh out, pack, ice and dispatch to the customers; filliters with razor sharp knives bone out prime fish for the restaurant trade. In a shed at one end of the market an oilskin-clad figure, indistinct in the billowing vapour, feeds a hissing, rumbling machine with a diet of dirty fish boxes, and in return for their slimy contents, it chucks them out again, clean and ready for reuse.

By mid afternoon the first mackerel boats will be returning loaded down if they have been lucky enough to locate a good shoal of fish. It's all rush and panic now to try and get the mackerel boats landed and their fish out of the way before the trawlers come in to land, as they might well be loaded down as well. It is just fish, fish, everywhere you look; a team packing and icing mackerel into two stone cartons ready to load onto a waiting lorry; pallets stacked high with boxes of trawl fish such as whiting, squid, plaice, monk and lemon-sole are trundled into the chill rooms to keep them in good condition for the following morning's auction. When a spell of fine weather coincides with a good run of fish, the pace for all concerned is relentless.

Among all the organised chaos of boats, men and fish, two wild animals, one very large and one very small, adopted the harbour as their own.

The large animal was a very fat one-eyed bull seal, later to be named Nelson, while the small animal was a feisty little cormorant that acquired the name of Kevin. Both creatures considered the whole shooting match was organised purely for their benefit, and while Kevin hated Nelson to the point where he would honk in fury at him from the safety of the quay, when the old boy sculled up to the market on the first of the flood tide, Nelson would turn his blind eye, ignoring Kevin completely.

This seal had knocked around the south Cornish coast for several years and was known in Newlyn, Falmouth and Mevagissey. Being a fairly intelligent animal he had obviously come to the conclusion that it was a lot easier to have fish thrown at him than hunt them himself. To this end he became quite tame and would hang around the quays trying to look cute and interesting. How 30 stone of battle-scarred blubber achieved that, I don't know, but he did; he charmed everyone, fishermen, market workers and visitors alike and he never ever went short of a meal. His appetite was prodigious. No matter how much fish was flung his way he never turned it down; any fish would do, but a conger was definitely his favourite. Floating on his back, holding one between his flippers, he would carefully skin it, then devour it with such obvious relish that it made you wonder if you shouldn't try raw conger yourself. Five stone of mackerel in one session was his record blow out, and he might have eaten more had there been more to give him. He seemed to bask in all the attention that he received and appeared to know his name, turning when called and posing endlessly for visitors to take his photo. Nelson made Looe his headquarters but would holiday at other ports now and then. During the breeding season he would decamp to the rocks around Looe Island, where passengers on the pleasure boats would observe him paying close attention to a lady friend. Skippers calling out to him would be rewarded with a look as if to say, "Bugger off, can't you see I'm busy?"

After a week or two his lust would be sated and a somewhat leaner Nelson would appear back in the harbour to resume gorging on fish and charming the people in equal measure. Once or twice, through mating battles or misjudging boats propellers, he received some nasty looking injuries and the state of Nelson's health would become of widespread concern, the local papers carrying the story. Endless worried well-wishers viewed him from the quayside, a specialist vet from the seal sanctuary at Gweek was summoned who

110

usually prescribed some tablets to be put in his fish. Once or twice, Kevin got hold of these doctored fish first and I often wondered exactly how he felt afterwards, a half stone bird swallowing a 30 stone seal's medicine. With an army of adoring fans, both locals and visitors, Nelson became something of a celebrity and his value as a one-animal tourist attraction was probably only rivalled by Fungi, the dolphin of Dingle Bay, Ireland.

But the limelight was not to be entirely his. For a while he had to share it, as well as some of his fish. The story of Kevin the cormorant began during a prolonged and severe winter gale sometime in the mid 1990s, when he was found starving and bedraggled, crouched down sheltering behind a curb on East Looe quay. Terry Puckey, one of the harbour staff, took pity and, scooping him up in his hands, took him down to the fish market and fed him a mackerel. Resting in a fish box out of the wind and weather, with a good meal down his neck, he soon made a recovery and for that he was then rewarded with more fish. And so another bright creature soon realised that here was a whole new way to live, never mind wasting energy swimming around the reefs after fish that really didn't want to be caught. No, waddle around the quay looking cute, and all the fish you can manage will be flung at you. Bingo, got it cracked!

And that is exactly what he did. The cheeky bird charmed the socks off everybody; he was irresistible. Swimming up river, he would hop up the steps by the war memorial and make all haste down to the fish market. With very short legs placed right aft on their bodies and little flippery feet, cormorants aren't built for running, but Kevin always did his very best. Legs going like pistons, feet slap, slap, slapping on the concrete, he would hurry down the quay looking like a portly little gentleman in an evening suit. And if, when the market came into view, somebody waved a mackerel to encourage him, he would try to go faster still, honking loudly in anticipation of a good feed. It was a wonder he didn't blow a gasket.

Kevin became very tame; you could sit down beside him and stroke his feathers which closer examination would reveal were not the dull brown cormorants always seem to look, but were iridescent, each feather edged with a cream coloured outline. If, upon his arrival at the market each morning, he was ignored because all hands were busy with the auction he would waddle over to Andrew Trust the auctioneer, there to firmly and persistently shake his trouser leg with his beak until eventually, as it becomes very difficult to concentrate or maintain your dignity with a hungry cormorant hanging off your trousers, Andrew had to call a brief halt to the proceedings while Kevin was given his breakfast.

Like Nelson the seal, Kevin the cormorant seemed to relish both the fish and the attention he received, posing with visitors while his photo was taken, but he always had an aura about him that he was your equal and not a pet. I think that both he and Nelson considered they had invested a lot of time and effort in taming and training humans, not the other way about as we thought, and looking back, maybe they were right. Together, but apart, this unlikely duo led the life of Reilly and entertained the public for several years. On one occasion Kevin failed to appear on the market for a week or more and everyone became very concerned for him. And then someone found a dead cormorant in the harbour: it had to be Kevin, and to show respect for his passing, a minute's silence was held in the market. But surprise, surprise, a couple of days later, to everyone's delight, the real Kevin appeared, not dead after all, and ravenous for his breakfast.

When his end did come it was very sad. For a long time he had been pushing his luck with Nelson; he would hover in the water off the seal's blind side, and when people flung him fish, the cocky little cormorant would dart ahead and snatch the fish from right under his nose. This trick drove Nelson to distraction, and on several occasions he caught Kevin by the tail and gave him a good ducking, but the bird just couldn't resist annoying the old seal. Then one day Nelson, ready to explode at the loss of his fish, grabbed Kevin by the wing and gave him one hell of a shaking. In great distress, he hopped up the nearest steps and more or less jumped up into the arms of one of the fish market workers, one wing dangling, broken and all but torn off. Kevin was rushed off to the vet, who declared his wing to be beyond any hope of repair, and as a one-winged cormorant could neither fly nor swim he would never survive. So the vet had to put him down, and a great little character was sadly gone from the harbour.

Nelson carried on as ever, posing for the public and consuming incredible amounts of fish, living many more years than he would have as a wild seal. But with age came infirmity; he started to lose the sight in his one good eye, eventually going blind. And that was his end. He groped around the quays, getting ever thinner, unable to see to feed or to dodge the boats. It was heartrending to witness, and there was nothing anyone could do about it. Nelson starved until he was about half his former size and one day, instead of going out to sea on the ebb tide, he swam up the river to haul out on a sand bank where he died.

But that wasn't the end of the Nelson story. During his years in Looe harbour he had become so well known and loved that a few years after he had passed on, funding was raised and a full sizes statue of him was modelled and cast in bronze. On a rock by the river side at West Looe, Nelson the seal, in effigy, still charms his public.

21

Wind Of Change

By the mid 1980s a chill wind of change was blowing from all points of the compass. The Maritime and Coastguard Agency was starting to introduce new rules and regulations for fishing boat safety, entailing expensive surveys, endless form filling and the buying of over-priced pieces of uselessness that were supposed to make your boat safe at sea. Good seamanship, common sense and years of experience now counted for very little unless your paperwork was in order.

Fish conservation schemes were being introduced, and the issuing of fishing licences had begun, limiting what species you could fish for and where and when, but none of it seemed to make any sense. Fish were not being conserved, just flung back dead if you weren't allowed to land them. Plus, every catch had to be recorded in a log book, and buff envelopes containing letters and forms printed on yellow paper dropped through the letter box on a daily basis, forever informing you of what you were and were not allowed to do. The fishing industry was being driven into a corner to be emasculated by bureaucracy.

Earning a living as a fisherman entailed very long hours and hard work in conditions that shore-side workers could never imagine. But the glory, if glory it was, of our way of life was the freedom and independence that we enjoyed. This made up for everything. The wet, the cold, the pitching rolling deck that was sometimes so bad that you spent the day working on your knees; the winter gales that kept you in harbour for weeks at a time while bills you couldn't pay piled up. It was all accepted as part of the way of life, but that life was ours and we led it as we saw fit. How I loathed and detested this outside interference.

But never mind there was always the summer passenger trade... or was there? It was around this time that the budget airlines started to make huge inroads into the domestic holiday market, flying millions of people away to exotic sun-filled foreign destinations for less money than it cost to holiday in Cornwall where, unfortunately, grey skies are as likely as blue. The good times were drawing to a close. It was now no longer feasible to employ two crewmen full time; Nezzer left to work on a trawler, while the Goat got a job ashore. I now worked the *Ibis* by myself in the summer time, taking out whatever sharking trips I could book up, plus the odd weekend taking divers out to the local wrecks and reefs when, for some reason, other skippers were reluctant to take them.

I enjoyed the shark angling. It was easy hours and good money with few expenses, and over the years I had the pleasure of meeting some very interesting people; there were never two days alike. People's experience of a day out sharking varied tremendously, depending on the weather conditions and the success rate with the sharks. Without doubt, venturing out to sea with a gang of novices when the weather was only just about workable was usually a recipe for utter misery. Anglers joining the boat at nine o'clock in the morning would be told that the forecast was not very good, and even though there was a fresh wind blowing it would rarely deter them. Bravado, I think, was the main driving force; nobody wanted to chicken out in front of the others and there was likely to be loads of bluster about how they had fished in a force nine out of Scarborough etc, and anyway, some would say, it was much more exciting when it was a bit rough. So away we would go, rise and fall, roll and plunge, spray flying, taught sheeted mizzen shivering in the breeze, while squally rain showers lashed from solid grey sky as we headed out to the sharking grounds, 12 or 15 miles off the coast.

Inevitably, after an hour of this kind of motion, a few of the intrepid band of anglers would now be quietly studying the horizon, a greenish waxy sheen playing on their rather unhappy faces.

"You feeling okay?" I would enquire.

"Yes, fine skipper, fine," they would lie. A little later, honking and gurgling noises would announce that homage was now being paid to Neptune. Fortunately, most people got to the lee rail in time

115

and made a good clean job of it. But for some, well, vomit went everywhere, over themselves and others, in the deck bucket, in the fish boxes, in carrier bags and the bag that held their packed lunch, or perhaps someone else's. It could be mayhem in the sick bay. By the time we reached the sharking grounds maybe half the passengers would be out for the count. Those remaining would insist that they were okay and wanted to carry on, so the boat would stop and lay broadside to drift to the wind and waves. The shark lines were baited up and streamed away and the fittest of the anglers, braced against the incessant rolling, jigged away with the boat rods to catch a few mackerel. But now came the real test: the 'rubby dubby'.

A dustbin lashed to the port rail, full of salted pilchards and mackerel, all soft and mushy, the crusty top layer seething with maggots. About two stone of this vile mixture was then decanted into a mesh bag and hung over the side to attract the sharks. The smell of it could take your breath away. Every time the bag was shaken to lay down the rubby dubby trail of fish oil and bits, a collective groan would go up from the anglers as the dreadful stench proceeded to envelope every corner of the boat. Those building up for a spew, or were spewing or who had just spewed, could well make up threequarters of the crew at this point, a far cry from the bold lads they had been but a couple of hours before. If they all agreed, then very often a day like that would be terminated with an early return to port, but if a few hard nuts insisted on staying, then so be it.

A shark on the line will buck every one up. Seasickness will be entirely forgotten while the fight lasts, but afterwards the dreaded *mal de mer* creeps back and once again a boatload of misery slowly rolls the hours away. Motoring back to harbour at the end of such a day, once the calm of the bay was reached, even those who hadn't moved all day would come back to life. And by the time we entered harbour, this sea-battered bunch would now be posing on the deck like Viking heroes, and why not? They had certainly earned it.

At the other extreme was the perfect day. There was one I recall on the *Ibis* that could not have been better if it had been scripted for a Walt Disney film. The weather was fine and bright, a light offshore wind ruffled a sea that sparkled in the sunlight and the anglers relaxed around the boat drinking tea and chatting. Never mind jumpers and oilskins, T-shirts were clothing enough on such a day. About five miles out we came across the biggest pod of killer whales that I had ever seen, about 60 as near as I could tally them. They seemed to be doing nothing more than sculling idly about with their great dorsal fins out of the water, so I stopped the boat and we watched them for a while. And what a show we had: they swam around the boat, dived under it or just lay alongside to have a look at us. It was a memorable sight, but the atmosphere around a pod of killers could be cut with a knife. It's as if they are saying 'keep your distance, don't annoy us or we will have you and your boat'. And that would be no idle threat; these animals are top predators, 30 to 40 feet long and their weight measured in tons. They are also highly intelligent.

Nudging the boat slowly and respectfully from out of their midst, we cruised away out to the sharking grounds. Once there, the lines were streamed away and the 'rubby' trail was laid. By lunch time we had caught three good-sized sharks and a box of mackerel on the feather lines. It was then that the dolphins appeared, a big pod of them, leaping, laughing and gambling all around the boat. The atmosphere with them was just so different from the killer whales: it was 'whoopee, what fun we are having, it's just so good to be alive'. For five minutes or so they entertained us royally, and then that was it; the show was over, and away they went, cutting along effortlessly at about 20 knots. Incredible animals.

A little later two more sharks took our bait. I was both surprised and delighted because sharks usually make themselves very scarce when dolphins are about. We arrived back in Looe that evening, everyone suntanned and happy, with many a tale to tell, cameras full of shark, whale and dolphin pictures. In all the years I took people out shark fishing there was never a day to equal that one. It was indeed the perfect day.

One other exceptional day took place in the spring of 1970 when I was relief skipper one Saturday on a little shark boat called the *Guiding Star*. The boat was booked by a gang of students who had never been out angling before. It was a windless day, grey and clammy, and I had intended to fish a good berth at the back of the Eddystone lighthouse but the fog clamped down thick and heavy and I stopped a berth inside of the lighthouse instead. In such conditions the advantage was two-fold: first, we would be safe from any shipping, and secondly, because we had no navigation equipment other than a compass in those days, the foghorn of the lighthouse would give a good bearing for home. The disadvantage was that it was not really an area you would expect to find many sharks, but I wasn't going to tell the students that.

We drifted along in a silent white world, the students entertaining themselves catching mackerel and whiting on the boat rods as the fog wrapped about us like a wet blanket. I was sitting in the wheelhouse enjoying a bite of lunch when a ratchet on one of the shark rods started to go click-click-click in a slow and measured way, indicating that probably a piece of seaweed or a lump of drift wood had caught under the float, for when a shark takes a bait the ratchet fairly screams into life. Handling the rod, I tightened the clutch to wind in and investigate the line when it went bar tight and I had to quickly slacken away again. I shouted to the students that we had a shark and swiftly one of them sat in the shark chair eager to take the rod. And with that, a damn great Mako shark broached the surface and then made off dolphin-like across the water, line screeching from the reel at a terrific rate.

Shouting to the anglers to pull the other lines in as quickly as they could, I started the boat's engine and chased after the shark at full throttle before it ran all the line off the reel. The next minute it was hard to starboard and we went astern as the shark dived. We now lay still on the water, watching the bar-taught vertical line cutting little patterns in the surface. The Mako was hard on the bottom jinking about trying to work out what its next move should be. Immediately the line went slack. The shark was coming up fast, and the angler wound his reel like a demon to retrieve the slack. Then suddenly, about 20 yards from the boat, this huge fish exploded clear out of the water like a Polaris missile. Landing with a mighty splash, it then took off into the fog, leaping and thrashing, desperately trying to escape its tormentors. At full throttle we chased off down the line after it, and again it dived to the bottom. With the engine burbling on tick-over, all eyes were riveted to the line, watching and waiting for the shark's next move. This was a once in a lifetime fish, and even with an experienced angler on the line, the odds of landing one of these monsters was not in our favour. A little bow wave squirted up the line as it cut around in the water, back and forth, in and out. Everyone's nerves were stretched as taught as that line. One mistake and it would be gone. The shark stayed on the bottom doing nothing, probably tired, so I told the lad on the rod to try to lift, drop and reel. This worked, and inch by inch up it came like a dead weight, exhausting work for the angler but he had to keep at it. I made the big flying gaff ready, but all the time I was expecting to dive for the throttle should the thing take off again. And then it was visible down in the water… up, up it rose, huge and powerful. Bloody hell, I said to myself, had I really got to risk life and limb driving a gaff into that. Laying dead in the water, it came to the surface right alongside the boat and just as I went to make with the gaff it erupted into life once more, an explosion of raw strength and fury.

I slammed the gaff down on the deck and jumped to the wheel and engine controls. It was game on again. The *Guiding Star*'s little cheapo engine was having the guts revved right out of it as we hurtled off after the shark. The battle raged on for nearly two hours, the shark diving and broaching and me never knowing from one second to the next which way the wheel would have to go. I had visions of us ramming another fishing boat or yacht as we charged madly about in the fog, looking at nothing but the angle of the line off the bow. Eventually the line was, yet again, up and down in the water, the shark hard on the bottom, resting. Just keeping the line tight I let the angler have a rest as well. He and the Mako were in about the same condition - knackered. Then it was back to business to see if we could bring it to the surface, slowly, lift, drop and reel, lift, drop and reel, inch by inch for an arm aching 40 fathoms. We were all staring down into the water in a state of nervous anticipation, knowing that there were still plenty of ways of losing this thing yet. And there it was, its great grey outline now visible a couple of fathoms down, she rose, she rose, now on the surface alongside the boat, quiet, and we hoped exhausted. This time it didn't explode back into life, so in went the flying gaff right up under the jaw. I twisted out the handle and pulled hard on the lanyard to bring this monster's head just clear of the water, then made fast. If it had come back to life now it could break the boat up, but no, it thrashed and banged around a bit but the fight seemed to have gone out of it. We had won the battle.

After ten minutes or so it lay still, tethered to the boat by the flying gaff lanyard, but now what were we going to do with it? It was much too big and heavy to get aboard the boat, so four or five lanyards had to be spaced out along its body and inch by inch, pulling on them in turn and making fast to the stringer, the Mako was lifted just clear of the water. When we got back to Looe, this great fish tipped the scales at 326 pounds, not a record breaker by any means, but by far the biggest fish I ever had anything to do with catching.

* * *

By 1988 the writing was on the wall. Because of the activities of the industrial boats, our main winter fishery, hand-lining for mackerel, had become much too precarious to make a season out of; trawling was now the only option. But against the powerful new boats then working out of Looe, the *Ibis* just couldn't compete at that game, so either I had to invest in a purpose-built trawler or get out of fishing. With the right boat and gear a very good living could be earned all year round with the trawl, but I just could not face the mind-numbing boredom of that trade, as well as being hemmed in on all sides by the new rules and regulations.

I used to wake in the mornings always looking forward to the new day, but by now it was all becoming a worry and a chore, and that is no way to lead your life. Come the spring paint up of that year, I retired the *Ibis* from commercial fishing. She had done 58 years on the trot, so maybe she was ready to retire. I had decided instead to concentrate on a more diverse summer trade: previously it had been shark fishing seven days a week, but that, like the winter mackerel fishery, was becoming much less reliable. Foreign holidays were reducing the number of people taking their holidays in the Westcountry and also, probably due to nature programmes on television, many people were becoming much more conservation-minded. Sharks were no longer viewed as evil monsters of the deep that deserved nothing better than to be fought by heroic anglers, dragged out of the water and killed, for that had been the attitude only a few years before. Now any that were caught were released back into the sea unharmed, and a good job too. The only trouble was that sharks were now being slaughtered in their thousands by large commercial fishing vessels, greatly reducing the numbers that came up the Channel. This meant that instead of being able to catch sharks on a daily basis almost anywhere off the coast, a shark angling boat might now go days without seeing one, so yet another of our seasons was under threat.

It was a similar story for the boats that took anglers out reef and wreck fishing for conger, ling, pollack etc. For now, most of the wrecks and all of the reefs and rough ground were being smothered with fleets' monofilament nets, and they killed just about anything that swam. Many of the more serious-minded fishing clubs from up country and the big angling organisations from Holland, Belgium and Germany that used to make block bookings with the Looe boats began to take their trade elsewhere because results with rod and line off the south Cornish coast had dropped off dramatically. It was all change and unfortunately non of it was for the better.

With the *Ibis* now stripped of all her fishing gear, I employed local shipwright Jeff Lewis to refit her for her new role. I had a deckhouse built over the fish room, inside which was a small galley and comfortable seating for the passengers. Two cabins were fitted in the fore peak, increasing the bunk space from five to eight and, to finish the job, I had her re-rigged with mast and sail. The *Ibis* and I were about to embark on a whole new career. My wife Margaret and I started doing sailing holidays to Brittany, the Channel Islands, the Scilly Isles and Ireland. The *Ibis* was a fine sea boat in any weather, especially with a rig of sail to keep her steady; many is the time we crossed the Channel with a force five to seven blowing. When we weren't on sailing charters, we were booked by diving clubs to explore the wrecks and reefs that lay off shore from Looe, and in addition we still did a certain amount of sharking if other bookings were a bit slack. Within a few years we had built up a very good trade, our customers for the diving and the sailing rebooking with us year after year. A good living could now be earned with the *Ibis* from May to September; the expenses were low and the enjoyment factor most of the time was high and, compared to commercial fishing, it was like being paid to go on holiday.

During the winter months the boat was de-rigged and sheeted down under tarpaulins. But time and tide, as the saying goes, wait for no man, and time was now rapidly overhauling the old *Ibis*. By the mid 1990s a new generation of dive charter craft was coming into service, high speed shiny things made of glass fibre with hydraulic lifts instead of a ladder to get the divers back aboard, while what was left of the shark fishing was now dominated by modern high speed angling boats. Another huge problem for an old vessel was being able to comply with the new rules and regulations that the MCA was then introducing for vessels carrying passengers.

If I wanted to keep the *Ibis* working, the only option that I could see was to give her a massive refit overseen by the MCA surveyors to convert her into a charter yacht, and that was an expense that I just could not contemplate.

The 2001 season drew to a close in late September when we returned home to Looe from a boisterous gale of wind charter to Brittany, laying the boat up for the winter as usual but not quite sure what our next move with her would be as a new MCA survey was due. To be honest, the writing was on the wall in capital letters, but I just didn't want to read it. I had now owned and worked the *Ibis* for 23 years, trawling, mackerel fishing, sharking, diving and sailing and she had never let me down, fine weather and foul. But now, after a working life of 71 years, her race was run, her day was done. It was time to retire her as a working boat.

Bob Cann, a friend of mine from Torbay, ended all the pondering with a phone call enquiring if the *Ibis* was for sale, as someone he knew wanted to buy a lugger. I had not said a word to anyone about selling up, so I was quite stunned by Bob's call, but at the same time I knew it was time I faced up to the reality. So I agreed to let this chap come and have a look at her and, to my surprise, within a week a deal had been done, the *Ibis* was sold and the money was in the bank, just as quick as that. My wife Margaret was tearful for days afterwards and I felt as miserable as if I had just betrayed a faithful old friend. It was all very sad and the end of a big part of our lives.

As usual, our customers had booked up their holidays and weekends on the *Ibis* for the following year, so I had to contact them all to tell them the news; it was such a hard thing to have to do because the Ibis had been a big part of their lives as well. Nick Jewson and his dive team from Bracknell in Berkshire had booked us for five or six weekends plus a couple of weeks every year for 16 years; even our newest dive club had been with us for over ten. We had been more or less fully booked for the coming summer, so I suppose you could say that we got out while the going was good.

22

Full Circle

Things seem to have gone full circle here in the port of Looe. Forty-five years ago when I first went to sea, most of the boats that took out angling parties in the summer months were laid up out of season because there was no winter fishery then for them to pursue. The men got jobs ashore painting and decorating, working in the building trade or whatever else might see them through until the following spring. These men were mostly middle-aged to elderly as there were few prospects for the younger men.

Then came the winter mackerel fishery and suddenly there was a good living to be had all year round. These good prospects brought the young men back into the trade. They worked hard, raised their families, bought their homes and new boats, and for over 30 years times were good and they prospered. Those young men are now themselves middle-aged and in the winter time they get jobs ashore painting and decorating, or on the buildings or whatever sees them through until the following spring. The great mackerel fishery that was once 400 boats strong county-wide, has ended and most of the men with the small boats are back where the previous generation had been 45 years ago.

The mighty shoals of fish that were once miles wide and as deep as the sea have now all gone, broken up and slaughtered for fish meal at rock bottom prices by huge purse seiners and mid water trawlers. A few boxes of hand-line caught mackerel are landed here and there, now and then and make very good money, to great acclaim by fishmongers, restaurateurs and food 'ponces' on television. "Wonderful quality fish from a sustainable fishery, bla.. bla.. bla…" they bang on. Meanwhile, out at sea, the industrial fishing ships are still slaughtering the pelagic fish as hard as they can go. The ever-decreasing shoals of herring, pilchard and mackerel are being located and wiped out. In these times of much trumpeted conservation measures, how can these vessels be allowed to continue? Even under the strictest control, they don't fish, they exterminate. Get these sea raping behemoths off the water and give the shoals of pelagic fish a decent chance to recover. And when they have done so, only then can there be such a thing as a sustainable fishery; hand-lining for mackerel and drift netting for herring and pilchards, fleets of small local boats landing good quality fish for human consumption. Then, once again, thousands would be employed as the ports and harbours, coves and quays all around the Cornish coast go from being picturesque and historic tourist traps, to being alive and vital once again, doing the job that they were designed to do, servicing a fishing fleet. Forty years ago, before the arrival of the purse seiners, we witnessed just such a revival, but sadly I doubt that it will happen again. For while the big fishing companies have money and influence, the slaughter will doubtless continue, at least until there is not enough fish left to sustain them, but by then they probably won't care. The big men would have made their fortunes and will have retired somewhere 'completely unspoiled'.

As for the Looe trawlers, for a variety of reasons their numbers have gone into decline, but it is now policy to reduce the fishing effort all around Europe. There used to be grants to build new boats; now there are grants to scrap them. Our fleet has shrunk to a dozen or so far from new boats, and most of the men who work on them, to put it politely, match their boats. Fishing has always been an industry of boom and bust, highs and lows. In my time it held good for a generation, but once again it seems to be in decline. Something has to be done to protect the fish stocks because with today's powerful modern boats and gear technology the assault on them can be relentless. I only hope that when it all balances out that the modern fishing industry doesn't become the sole domain of a few all-powerful fishing companies. Because for so many reasons, the small men operating from the historic coves, ports and harbours all around our shore must survive. There is nothing so sad and soulless as a fishing harbour without any fishing boats. Pay a visit to Mousehole in west Cornwall or Cameret in Brittany and you will understand what I mean. On the walls of the harbour-side pubs and restaurants hang those beautiful black and white photos taken a generation or so ago, showing a busy haven, crowded with working craft plying their many different trades, all now ghosts and echoes from the past, while today's reality is the yachts and pleasure boats that occupy the moorings, their sterile, artificial ambiance only serving to amplify the tragedy that has overtaken these places.

23

The Future

During my lifetime here in Looe, I have seen the fishing fleet change completely three times. From a handful of worn out luggers, plying their age old trade with drift nets and long lines, to a fleet of 40 mackerel boats, and then to a harbour full of trawlers.

The luggers, many of them now well over a hundred years old, still exist as much cherished classic sailing craft while the mackerel boats, barring a very few, have all completely disappeared. Where those hundreds of boats went I have no idea. It seems just like a conjuring trick to me; somebody muttered an incantation, waved a wand and hey presto, they were gone. Now, standing more or less alone in every port, are the trawlers, so successful that they were on their way to reducing much of the seabed to a wasteland. But their numbers have been greatly reduced and conservation measures are coming into being, aimed at reversing the damage done and reviving the fish stocks. In the short term, the fishermen are probably going to suffer (yet again) but hopefully, in the long term, providing the conservationists don't insist on making a pet out of every fish, then the fishermen should see some benefits. I certainly hope so.

I think we must be optimistic. High quality fish restaurants have opened up everywhere, cooking fish dishes of all kinds; even the humble pilchard, now remarketed as a Cornish sardine has found favour. The once despised mackerel is now fussed over for its omega three oils etc, and a couple of fillets of it cooked and served with a bit of salad can cost more than a fisherman would have been paid for a five-stone box of them not many years ago. To make a living, a fisherman once had to be up to his knees in fish because for most of the time they didn't make very much money but times have changed, thank goodness. The emphasis is now on quality, not quantity; on fish being fresh and locally caught. Nothing boosts the feel-good factor for diners in a restaurant than the sight of a fisherman delivering a box of his day's catch fresh to the kitchen door. It underlines everything that today's chefs stand for and what they are trying to achieve.

Maybe this is the future for the fishermen in our small coves and harbours - not to be lumped in on the market with the big boats' catches as happened years ago, but to be appreciated for being small, being local and landing top quality fish. Whether a diner in a restaurant can tell if his monkfish was landed by a beam trawler or from a small local netter is not the point; people are prepared to pay for the provenance of their food and trust that it is fresh and locally caught. And on this, a whole new branch of the fishing industry is developing. I once asked some of our leading fish merchants if the catch from a sailing fishing vessel would command any premium? They all seemed confident that if such a vessel was working many restaurants would be prepared to pay well over the odds for its fish, simply because of the provenance that it would carry. So, as always the fishing industry is changing, never because it wants to but always because it has to. What the next generation of fishing boats in Looe will look like and how they will operate, only time will tell. A small fleet of trawlers will probably survive if conservation measures and fuel costs don't wipe them out. But if, in time, the measures we are threatened with prove to be successful and the men are allowed to fish these areas again, then maybe we shall see a growing fleet of boats going back to more passive ways of fishing, using hand lines, long lines and static nets, methods that don't smash up the ground or kill spawn and immature fish. But who knows what the future will hold.

Epilogue

Now in retirement, I haven't given up the sea, and while I still enjoy good health I don't intend to. My wife Margaret and I bought the 38 foot lugger *Erin* back from Brittany. She had been built in Mevagissey in 1904 and fished from that port until 1976. Gerard Sey of Lézardrieux then bought her poor worn-out old hull and breathed life back into it, sailing her around the Breton and Cornish coasts for the next 28 years before offering her for sale in 2004.

We gave her a good thorough refit and now, from April to October, we cruise in her all around the coast of the south west, from Torbay to the Scilly Isles and from the Channel Islands to the Gulf of Morbihan.

Cruising a boat for your own pleasure is such a vastly different experience from operating one to earn a living with. You can take your time, and haven't got to go out when the weather is inclement, but we still do get caught out every now and then, but that's life. We visit many of the ports and harbours that I knew in my fishing days, meeting old friends from those times. But all the hustle and bustle has gone from them. Whether it's commercial or pleasure fishing, where once there were fleets of each, now there are just a few, and the dreaded marina forever encroaches as more harbours turn to the yachtsman for their salvation, for what else can they do? Even Newlyn, the monarch of all Cornish fishing ports, has put out the welcome mat because their once mighty fishing fleet looks to be heading for the buffers.

Will white plastic hulls and smartly attired yachtsmen be the only form of life in our harbours in years to come? Will old photos, framed and hung in the pubs and restaurants, be the only record of what once was? This has been the fate of so many ports in Brittany. I just hope that here in Cornwall a balance can be struck.

Glossary

AMIDSHIPS: Mid section of a vessel.

AFT: Stern section of a boat.

ABEAM: To come level with another vessel.

BAIT-UP: The required amount of mackerel or pilchard to make bait for a line.

BEAM: Width of a vessel across the deck at her widest point.

BACKSTAY: Part of a masts standing rigging.

BAULKS: Large beams of timber.

BELAYING: Making fast or tying off.

BEND ON: To tie two ropes together.

BENDS: Heavy oak timbers to reinforce the hull of a boat.

BIGHT: A loop of rope.

BILGE: Bottom of a boat in the mid section.

BITTER END: The very end of a coil of rope.

BRIDLES: Part of the rigging of a trawl.

BULWARKS: The extension of the hull above the deck to stop fish, gear and crew from going overboard. On a lugger this was set at knee height.

BULKHEAD: A partition on a boat.

BUTT: Formed by two planks meeting end to end on a frame.

CABIN SOLE: Cabin floor.

CAPSTAN: Mechanical device to haul ropes and cables.

CARVEL: Planking method where planks lay edge to edge.

CAULKING: To pack seams of planks with a waterproof material to prevent leaking.

CLEAT: A device for securing a rope.

CLINKER: A method of planking a boat where the plank edges overlap.

CLUCKY DOWN: Down on your haunches like a hen in a nest.

COAMINGS: The frame around a deck opening, usually 10 or 12inches higher than the deck itself.

COD-END: The very end of a trawl net where the catch gathers.

DANN: A buoy used to mark the end of a net, a long-line or a fleet of crab pots. A flag is fixed to it.

DEADWOOD: Baulks of oak laid between keel and sternpost and keel and stem to add strength.

DECK WASH: Sea water pumped to a hose on the deck for washing down.

DIGGING OUT: Pumping a boat by hand.

DRAG: To tow a trawl.

DRAUGHT: Depth of hull from waterline to keel.

FAIRLEAD: A guide to keep rope in position over a boat's rail.

FATHOM: 6 feet.

FOOTROPE: A heavy rope wound with chain tied to the bottom half of a trawl mouth to make ground contact.

FOREPEAK or CUDDY: Small cabin in the bow of a boat.

FRAMES: Inside skeleton of vessel that carry the planks, usually made of oak.

GUNNELS OR GUNWHALES: The top outside rail of a boat.

GURDIE: A V-rimmed wheel mounted on a stanton, used to work a fishing line.

HEADROPE: Upper rope on a fishing net.

HITCH: A class of knot.

HOVELLER: A boatman who transports goods and personnel to ships anchored off a harbour.

JIB: Triangular sail set between mast head and bowsprit.

JOWTER: Fish seller, usually working from a van or a cart.

KEEL: Heavy elm or oak baulk, forming the backbone of a boat.

KEVEL: A stout oak bar bolted across two stanchions to make a strong point for mooring ropes.

KNOTS: Speed of a vessel through the water, based on a nautical mile of 2000 yards.

LANYARD: Length of rope tied to a bucket or fender.

LEE: Down wind.

LEG: A stout baulk of timber shaped to fit the up and down shape of a boat amidships. This is to prevent a vessel going over on her side at low tide when working from a drying harbour.

LUFF: Front or leading edge of a sail.

MIZZEN: Aft mast sail on a fore and aft rigged vessel.

OTTER BOARDS: A device for keeping trawl gear spread while being towed.

PARTING BOARDS: Boards eight or ten inches in height set fore and aft on the deck to prevent the catch from sliding about.

PEAK: The top most part of a sail.

PELAGIC FISH: Shoaling fish such as mackerel, pilchards or herring

QUARTERS: The port and starboard aft sections of a boat.

RAIL: Reinforced timber around the top of a baot's hull.

RUDDER: Steering device at stern of boat.

SCRY: News of the whereabouts of a shoal of fish.

SCUPPERS: The gap between the deck and bulwark to allow drainage of sea water.

SHARPIE MIZZEN: Triangular shaped sail set at stern of boat.

SHEAR LINE: The line of a boat running fore and aft at the deck or rail.

SHEET: A tackle to control a sail.

SIDEWINDERS: Trawlers that haul and shoot their gear over the side as against the modern method of over the stern (stern draggers).

SPELL: A rest or breather.

STAUNCH UP: To swell the planking of a wooden boat when it has dried out.

STEM: The very front part of the bow, linking the keel to the deck and carrying the plank ends.

STERNPOST: An oak post linking keel to deck, carrying the transom or, if a double ender, the plank ends.

THWARTSHIPS or THWART: Side to side of a vessel or a seat running across a boat.

TRANSOM: The flat stern of a vessel, usually made of oak.

WARPS: Wire rope running from a trawler's winch to the sea bed for towing a trawl.

WATERWAYS: The narrow part of the deck between the net room coamings and the rail.

YARN: To talk or tell a story.

The Author

Paul Greenwood was born in Looe in 1947, the eldest of four children. His father Peter was a shipwright by trade, later to become an antique restorer; his mother Pamela was a schoolteacher. Paul went to sea at the age of 16, joining the lugger *Iris* in 1964 as a very seasick 'boy', working drift nets for pilchards and long lines for conger, ray and turbot. In the late 1960s he left the *Iris* to sail as bosun aboard the *Malcolm Miller* before returning to fishing in 1973. He bought his own boat, the lugger *Ibis*, in 1978 which he used for commercial fishing and later charter work with his wife, Maggie, until 2002. His first book, *Once Aboard A Cornish Lugger*, was published in 2007. Paul and Maggie now live in East Looe and spend their summers cruising in their 1904 lugger *Erin*.

Acknowledgements

Photographs reproduced by kind permission of Phil Lockley (cover picture), David Butters, Ivor Toms, Kevin Faulkner and the author.